W9-BFQ-983

The Joys of Woodstoves & Fireplaces

The Joys of Woodstoves & Fireplaces

Heating and Cooking with Wood

by Mary Presper

Illustrations by Tom O'Sullivan

Publishers · GROSSET & DUNLAP · New York
A FILMWAYS COMPANY

38977

*To my mother, now nearer ninety than eighty,
who with good humor can reminisce about the
rigors of "yesterdays," recognize the realities of "today,"
and relish with enthusiasm the "tomorrows."*

Acknowledgments

I welcome this opportunity to express my appreciation to family and friends who, to speak in metaphor, kept the fire burning during the days of drudgery in the preparation of this book. The gathered information often became so technical that to carry the message many times the "fire" was nearly put out. And there were times I seriously considered using this manuscript as kindling. I sincerely hope the efforts of my research and interpretation provides useful and functional information that can be read with more happiness than heaviness.

In the development of the recipes I wish to give special thanks to friends who literally were firetenders, logcarriers, assistant cooks and long-suffering guinea pigs. During the early recipe tests some of the sampled food was downright inedible (scorched, burned, undercooked and "ugh"). Thank you, one and all, for coming back for more!

Contents

The Joys of Woodstoves & Fireplaces

Introduction

I have written this book in order to share and revive the special pleasures centered around woodstoves and fireplaces, which I enjoyed as a child. These were everyday experiences, accepted as a way of life, which provided us with enjoyment and a warmth that not only thawed our hands and feet, but made our hearts secure as well. In the mornings, we would waken to the rattles and clanging of metal being stirred in the woodstove. In the evening, we would sit around the fireplace, hypnotized by its flickering flames. The old adage "A warm hearth makes a warm home" was never more truthful.

Lying in a warm bed in a very cold room on a recent midwinter visit to friends who have a year-round retreat in the New Hampshire hills, I found my thoughts drifting with nostalgia to those early days. My friends have a small old house with most of today's conveniences, along with some early inconveniences, even to the outhouse! But, best of all, they have wood heat, which they get from both a potbelly stove and a parlor stove. There is a register in every bedroom upstairs, which can be opened in the morning when the fires are started and the clanging starts below.

Waking in that New Hampshire house to the rattling of the stove jogged childhood memories. I could just smell the aroma of burning balsam infiltrating under the covers as I snuggled down on a winter morning at my grandmother's farmhouse in the hill country of Pennsylvania. The whistling of the teakettle signaled that the fire downstairs was hot enough for me to make a mad dash, grab my clothes (as well as the sock with the now-cold brick which had warmed my bed the night before), and run to dress in front of the open oven door of the kitchen range. I remember taking a dipper of water (still warm from the banked fire of the previous night) out of the stove reservoir, so I wouldn't have to wash in cold water. Then I would pull on my socks that had dried by the open oven door overnight and my high-top boots coated with neat's-foot oil to make them waterproof.

Grandmother served a wonderful breakfast of sour-milk or buttermilk pancakes (buttermilk from her churn); in the wintertime, it was buckwheat pancakes for extra warmth and energy. She always mixed the batter the night before, allowing it to ripen on the back of the stove or on the warming shelf above the stove's surface. The pancakes were baked on a soapstone griddle, then served with homemade butter slathered on top. There were fried apple rings made from apples harvested the previous fall, cored, cut into rounds, and strung on a line in the attic to dry. The apples were soaked overnight in water to regain some of their original moisture before being quick-fried in just a small amount of fat and sprinkled with brown sugar and cinnamon. They were slightly caramelized and had a wonderful flavor. In addition to these delicacies, my grandmother also served sausage patties, made from the ground and spiced meat of the pigs slaughtered in the fall. And, of course, we had real maple syrup (from the March "sap-run" of the farm's maple trees). The adults drank freshly ground coffee, while we chil-

dren had hot chocolate, though we might have a bit of coffee mixed in it if we wanted. Even so, there was a teakettle and a teapot of strongly steeped brew available on the back of the stove at all times.

While my grandmother didn't profess to be a short-order cook, the dexterity with which she wielded the pancake turner, skillets, and other utensils at the range would have overqualified her for the job. Watching her get that breakfast together was, in our youthful eyes, like watching a magician at work. We vied with one another as to who got the first bakeoff from her soapstone griddle. There was always a test pancake, baked first, and if browned just right and cooked through properly, one of us would usually get it.

My country grandmother happened to be a superb cook. She never restricted herself on any of the qualities or quantitites of foods that she used in her recipes. But she was also a very practical and thrifty person, being from a French and European background. She always had a soup pot simmering on the back of the stove, and on Saturday (which was "bake" day), the soup was particularly superb, having had all week to collect "stock" flavored with bones from roasts, chickens, meats, and leftover vegetable trimmings. What she would do was simmer all of these, keep them hot, season them with herbs and spices, and bring the soup to a boil at least once a day to keep down any germs, spoilage, or souring that might occur. And though Saturday was the best soup day, we were always permitted to go to the soup pot whenever we wanted a warm "bite." And what a wonderful (nutritious) bit that was for children coming in from outdoors, or to stay the healthy appetites of family members working out on the farm so they'd hold until the evening meals.

The fireplace was the center of our lives. Very often we cooked in it. A table would be set up where mother, with great flourish, would serve the foods cooked in the fireplace. We usually took part in the preparation of the meal. The foods were not especially exotic—just our ordinary fare—but what fun it was!

As children, when we wanted to snack, we had no hamburger shop nearby; we went home and gathered around the kitchen stove and made "treats." There was always a wheel—or a section of a wheel—of "store cheese" at home. We were permitted to cut from the wheel whatever amounts we wanted. We usually took two-inch squares (or a bit larger), put them on two-pronged, long-handled forks, removed the lids from the kitchen range, and toasted the pieces of cheese by holding them close, but not too close, to the embers. We were extremely careful not to spill any of that melted cheese on the range, because nothing smells worse than scorched cheese!

Grandmother spoiled her children and her children's children, there was no doubt about it. We were always allowed to go to the range, especially on cold days, to make our own hot chocolate with the melted chocolate grandmother kept in a bowl near the teakettle. Sometimes we removed the top of the kettle and set the bowl inside to melt the chocolate above the boiling water. We then scooped the melted chocolate into another, deeper, bowl and

using an old-fashioned Dover egg-beater beat hot milk into the mixture and sweetened it with sugar. When especially rich hot chocolate was wanted, we would also beat in an egg. It was the very best hot chocolate, the real thing!

We also cooked outdoors in both summer and winter. I remember many summers and springs going to our fishing camp along Pine Creek in Pennsylvania. There, in the mornings, my uncle and others caught trout in the stream and brought them to the house all ready to be rolled in cornmeal and cooked in a frying pan over the hot campstove for breakfast. Or we would bring the fish in, wrapped in ferns, Indian style, and put each one on a heated hot brick to bake in the oven for about a half-hour, always careful to have the bricks on a tray so the moisture and fish juices wouldn't drip onto the oven's deck and cause rust.

In the wintertime, we went cross-country skiing (in the dawn of the cross-country skiing days). Our skis had only toe straps, no fancy bindings, and if we wanted to go up and down mountains, we had to herring-bone or parallel-climb one step at a time up them since there were no ski lifts. Many times we would go through forests and groves of trees. Quite often we cooked our meals out.

Our "stove" was any old hollow tree stump that was about the right height, in which we built a fire with pine cones, twigs, and fallen limbs, etc., gathered nearby. If the snow was especially deep, we would kick off our skis, turn them upside down and make a sort of catwalk or platform in front of the stump. Our coffee or hot chocolate was then made in a beat-up coffeepot (always carried along on our trips) with clean snow scooped out from below the surface level. We would also cook steaks or other high-protein, portable foods, such as cheese and pemmican (a concentrated food made of beef, flour, molasses and suet), which would keep for at least a half a day. We even carried eggs, and to keep the shells from breaking, packed them in cornmeal or flour, which was also used to make "johnny cake."

I remember all those times with a great deal of joy. The fondest recollections of my early days center around the fireplace at home. In fall, winter, and spring there was always a cozy fire in the hearth. It was customary to spend the evening around the fireplace, reading poetry or literature of some sort, listening to mother play the piano, and, when I was little, drinking hot, spicy, mulled cider. Later, as a teen-ager, I was permitted to have a glass of sherry or port wine, as I dreamed in front of the flames. I made many memories around the wood fires in my home. I know you will, too.

16

Rediscover the Fireplace and Woodstove

It comes as no surprise to anyone that the sale of woodburning stoves in the last couple of years is booming. One reason, of course, is the energy crisis which has made people aware that wood as a fuel is both efficient and replaceable! As much as 50 to 75 percent of the heating bills in today's homes can be reduced by proper woodburning appliances!

An added advantage to using wood is the flavorful foods that can be prepared in these old-time appliances. Believe it or not, almost every food you can make with today's kitchen equipment could have been prepared on one of the original woodburning home ranges! Today, many gourmet cooks are turning to fireplace cooking and wood-cooking stoves for unique flavors.

The enjoyment we get psychologically and physically from the warmth of an open fire must, I have often thought, be inherited from that long-ago time when man first discovered the value of a controlled fire for keeping him warm and making his food more palatable. Man burned wood then, as he burns it now, and the source still remains! With proper management of woodlots, and lumbermen's proper technique of cutting from forests only a certain amount each year, so that growth is continuous, the source of wood supply as fuel should last as long as the world. Wood is the only fuel available that replenishes itself.

Furthermore, the burning of wood and the ashes that result cause less pollutants in the air and earth than any other fuel! In fact, nutrients are returned to the earth by decaying wood and ashes. These ecological plusses are in themselves enough to turn one back to wood for fuel!

Last, and assuredly not least, is the special sense of sociability that people feel sitting around a fireplace or close by a kitchen woodstove. The attraction of the fire, and the companionship of sharing it, make it a focal point of entertaining. (Doesn't everyone get up to add a log or poke an ember?) And once you have mastered cooking with wood—not at all difficult with the right tools and a bit of know-how—you and your hearth will be the star attractions for many an evening's home entertainment.

And let's not forget all those marvelous "smells" of woodfires—a unique bonus. At my grandmother's, we always saved the rind of oranges, grapefruits, and lemons. Some of these citrus rinds were stuck with whole cloves, and all were placed directly on the surface of the back of the stove to dry out. Their fragrance wafted through the house, permeating every room. Also, those citrus rinds, when they were dried out, were great to use as part of the kindling to help start the fires.

If we were having company, I remember the shovel, which was ordinarily used to take out the ashes in the cookstove, was placed in, or suspended slightly above, the stove embers. When it was very hot, some coffee beans were sprinkled in it and heated until they gave off that wonderful aroma of roasted coffee. At this time, my mother would hold the shovel of hot coffee beans aloft and quickly walk through the house, going into the parlor and the sitting room and through the entrance hall. This was done mostly in wintertime when the house and rooms were not often opened to the cold air of winter. Sometimes mother would heat the shovel on top of the range, place some sugar in it and some whole cloves. Just when the sugar slightly turned color and gave off that sweet caramelized odor, mingled with the clove fragrance, she would carry this concoction through the rooms. In those days, these were the only kinds of pleasant room deodorizers.

Of course, in many parts of the country, a woodstove or a fireplace, when properly exploited, is an invaluable ally against the weather. Today's homes rely on central heating plants, rather than fireplaces for warmth, and most people use either gas-fired or electric ranges for cooking. And even an oil-fired furnace or water heater relies on electric motors! Some homes are totally dependent on electricity for heat and cooking. Yet there are still areas of the country where there are power failures due to bad weather conditions—to summer storms as well as winter hazards. Then a household is left both cold and hungry. It is then that a wood fire comes to the rescue—proving itself man's friend—as it has through the ages. Today, countless people are installing "auxiliary" woodstoves and fireplaces, recognizing that they offer utilitarian value as well as romantic atmosphere and charm!

Origins of the Oven

The art of baking—and roasting—food in some sort of oven can be traced back to prehistoric man. Tribal man practiced early community cooperatives by sharing ovens placed outside the homes—either in the open or in buildings designated for cooking. Even in colonial Virginia such a practice was common. Individual housewives who were without the use of a neighborhood utility eventually found it more practical to have their "head of the house" build what was called a kitchen oven in a part of the fireplace. The term *kitchen oven* was used to differentiate this kind of oven from those located outside the home in both England and New England.

Kitchen ovens had the actual fires built in them, where they burned for a fairly long time and until the bricks or stones were thoroughly heated. Before using them, the ovens were swept clean of coals. The food was then placed in them to be baked, starting with breads (that took greater heat and a long time to bake), and tapering off with foods that required less intense heat. Kitchen ovens were also very useful in the preparation of meats and poultry that could be roasted slowly.

It is undoubtedly from these ancient origins, and through traditions and societal habits long established, that the term "Life around a warm hearth makes for a happy home" becomes a visual needlepoint hanging in the recess of our minds and a spur to the present boom of wood as a fuel.

In a marketing and consumers' list for 1976, there were more than a dozen major national distributors across the United States for "woodburning cook stoves," which ranged in price from $100 to $550.

19

As of November 1978, it was projected that by year's end, some 150,000 stove units would have been sold at a gross of $35 million dollars! Growth is further dramatized by the fact that in 1975 there were 164 manufacturers of woodstoves, while today there are over 500! The top of the wood-range line remains the Atlantic Queen, still being manufactured and sold at a starting figure of nearly $750. That price, of course, is only the beginning, stripped-down figure for this Cadillac of the kitchen. With certain added features, the cost of it can go to over one thousand dollars! When it gets to that price, many people can, and do, sell the baby grand piano, preferring comfort and cook-alongs to sing-alongs.

Dr. Franklin's Stove

Benjamin Franklin really initiated the beginning of the woodstove era in this country, although progress in that direction was already evident in Europe. Peasants in Russia slept warmly on top of indoor clay ovens, absorbing the heat that permeated through the walls. The Germans devised a method of using a single fireplace to heat two rooms with a metal plate, instead of a brick backwall (one plate constructed on each side of the wall); by heating the air and circulating naturally, this method revolutionized home heating, and the iron woodstove came into existence.

The fire in Franklin's Pennsylvania fireplace was started in a metal container set into a masonry wall. Outdoor air was channeled in and directed into a central heating chamber. Smoke and hot gases from the fire were then pulled below the hearth before being drawn up behind a brick false fireback, from whence it circulated the heat equally throughout the room.

Although the modern version of the stove (which is popularly labeled Ben Franklin) varies from the original design, it is a tribute to Dr. Franklin, whose great innovations in the development of conveniences and comfort rank among his many contributions.

When I was a little girl, smoke and hot gases were not the only thing that passed through the Pennsylvania Franklin fireplace that was in my grandfather's house: grandpop would send secret coded messages to me, carried by the thin metal sheet plate on each side of the wall. He disguised his voice and spoke of himself as "Dick." I confided in Dick, confessing to the forbidden things I had done, without ever realizing that it was grandpop on the other side of the wall.

Points to Check before Buying a Woodstove

Before you think about buying a woodstove, it is important for you to be fully aware of certain guidelines and purchasing principles.

1. When you buy a woodstove, safe construction is vital! While some stoves made in Taiwan and Japan are safe, quite a number are not. All foreign makes of woodstoves don't have the Underwriters' testing that is so important. It costs a manufacturer about $20,000 to $40,000 to have his products tested and given the approved label. The Underwriters Laboratories and the National Association of Fire Prevention performs these tests and either sanctions a seal of approval or not. It is really worth the manufacturer's cost to have this done. And if you are buying a woodstove, be sure that it is one of the approved ones—most of the American stoves usually carry the label.

2. Decide on the main purpose of the stove. Is it for heat or for cooking? The circulation and direction of the heat are different in each—not to mention the differences in design and engineering.

The interior design of cookstoves differs from that of woodstoves mainly in the additional drafting system which is built in to provide hot air around the oven. Therefore, models of cookstoves with ovens are more complex. However, many woodstoves can be adapted for cooking easily, with no design change other than the acquisition of flat tops with one or more removable lids for supplementary cooking.

3. Determine what size stove to buy. Will the stove be heating a small one-room area or serving as supplementary heating for the whole house? It is better to buy a slightly larger stove than is needed,

as it will be easier to operate it at a dampened or lessened heat output than to push a smaller stove to higher heat capacity.

Fuel efficiency is of major importance. There are too many variables in the vast numbers and designs of woodstoves to rate them on a fuel-efficiency basis. Factors that influence the heat output are: dampers in stovepipes, the number of elbows used, and the length of pipes as well as the kinds and dryness of the wood used.

4. An airtight stove is a requirement for fuel efficiency. Most Scandinavian stoves are airtight, but not all American ones are. For example, the cast-iron box stoves such as the potbelly, the parlor, or Franklin-style stoves are not completely airtight, while the Ashley, Kickapoo, and the Scandinavian ones such as the Tyrola and Jøtul *are* airtight and therefore about twice as efficient.

5. Manufacturers stress the importance of full draft control so that the fuel will burn slowly and completely, thus forming the least creosote build-up in the flue. Draft control is a vital factor for even heat distribution. Some stoves are equipped to permit you to "bank" the fire and maintain it for as long as 18 hours. The fire can even be extinguished and the unburned fuel relit when desired. These stoves provide long-term economy and are well worth the extra few dollars in initial cost.

The phrase *bank a fire* means (1) to deposit unburned logs on top of a fire and (2) to regulate it with draft controls in such a way that it burns slowly and steadily.

When you are able to bank a fire properly, consider yourself as having graduated from the minute waltz to a full concerto, as if playing a piano. There is nothing more disastrous nor discouraging than to find a fire that you thought properly banked to be completely burned out, or that the fire is completely snuffed out. There is great satisfaction to look in on a banked fire several hours later to discover it is still burning well. A banked fire that lasts overnight is indeed a great pleasure. Being able to adjust the draft and the dampers in a wood-burning fire is important.

Draft and damper control is especially important if you're planning to burn coal. And some wood stoves *do* burn coal. They have a grate that flips over and can be used either for wood or for coal, the narrower openings accommodating wood. When using coal, it is imperative to have a truly airtight stove, because the fuel burns in a confined area, and you must be certain that carbon monoxide gases go up the chimney and not into the room.

6. It is important to note the type of grate in the firebox and whether or not there are fire bricks lining the firebox wall. A grate that is too wide lets many embers fall through; also it lets too much air through, causing

the fire to burn too fast. A grate in which the openings are too close does not let enough air through.

When buying a modern stove that has no grate, it is important to make sure that it is lined with firebrick for maximum safety, as the wood is burned from the top down. Flues on these stoves are designed to recirculate gases so that they are thoroughly burned up instead of being drawn up through them.

Cast Iron or Steel?

Old timers believed there was no substitute for the quality offered in a cast-iron stove. This is not true today. There are cast-iron stoves which are actually of thinner metal and not as sturdily constructed as some heavy sheet metal stoves.

*

Whether to select cast iron over steel really depends on the thickness of the steel you want. Cast iron can crack, but it also has a longer life and retains heat longer. Steel bends and can develop leaks along the joining seams, but a stove of heavy steel should have a long life expectancy. Both metals rust and corrode, especially if overheated or when stored in damp areas.

*

Sheet metal is the least safe of all material used in construction and has a shorter life, whereas thick-plate steel is considered by some to be the safest bet. Thick-plate steel, however, can be quite expensive in contrast to cast iron, the most commonly used material, which is inexpensive and durable.

*

For quality guidelines check the following:
- Absence of air leaks and good joining of seams.
- Fitting of doors and tops should be tight.
- Is the stove lined or unlined? If unlined, what type of insulation is used—sand, firebrick, asbestos? A double metal wall with an air chamber is best.
- Be aware of the thickness of the metal used. Compare weights under consideration.
- How easy is it to load the stove?

The Woodstove Market

In general, it is wise to select new stoves from well-known manufacturers. Many distributors rate the top of the line to about five main stove manufacturers. In the order of their importance and availability across the country, they are: Monarch, Atlantic, Ashley, Sierra, and Tyrola.

One of the best publications for a current source of information and register of stove retailers and other wood-heat appliances is a yearly issue of the national sourcebook, *Woodstove, Fireplace and Equipment Directory*, put out by Energy Communication Press, Capitol Distributing Company, Charlton Building, Derby, CN 06418. This paperback is available on newsstands at $2. ($2.50 by mail, from the publisher.)

Here is a selection of new stoves offering special features that may fulfill your requirements:

Lanco's Early American Franklin Heater is based on Ben Franklin's stove and includes one all-purpose cast-iron grate in addition to a single iron boot (a cast-iron elbow at the rear to be attached to the flue or stovepipe) with damper control. An interchangeable top can easily adapt it for cooking, and the chimney openings are in the rear.

Greenbriar Products, Inc., claims to have improved the heat efficiency of the Franklin-type woodstove with its Fireplace/Stove, a very modern looking stove. The hearth on this model is made of firebrick, while the fire chamber is constructed of steel. Options on this stove include either a steel door with an air-intake grill or alternate door with heat-tempered glass, through which the fire is visible.

The Parlor Stove, by Lanco, is cast iron and features two large doors, a lift top for top-loading and a standard flat black finish. All models of this Parlor Stove are the same size and shape, and all can be loaded with fuel from the top, front, and side. These are elegant stoves that are not only decorative, but practical, since they radiate a great amount of heat. All casting from which the Parlor Stoves are made are original hand-carved patterns.

The Lanco Colony is an attractive, real wood-burning fireplace/stove with a two-way heating air circulator that finds its source in the Flow-Thru double walled construction. A 1½-inch air space is made in between a 12-gauge inner wall and a 16-gauge steel outer wall. Cold air enters from the floor, is heated as it passes up through the Flow-Thru system, then is recirculated into the room. Heat is also radiated from the surface of the free-standing fireplace, thus warming the air and cooling the unit's outer skin, a distinct advantage in that persons or small children nearby cannot be burned by accidental contact.

The Flow-Thru system is capable of heating 1,600 square feet of floorspace or a 40-by-40 square-foot area. This is a handy unit for frosty nights! The center-opening double doors mean easier and safer loading of logs up to 24 inches in length, and the expanded steel grate can be used with coal as well as wood. The stove also has a special ash-drop for easy

cleanup, and a tempered thermoglass fireplace enclosure that saves fuel.

A reasonably priced smaller stove is the Birchwood, by Lanco. It is one that will burn anything in the way of wood. The stove's top, bottom, front, and the firebox are made of heat retaining cast iron. This model also features a nickel-plated swing top, face plate, front legs, and shaped rails. The sidewalls are of heavy sheet steel.

The Kitchen Heater Model 4P is another versatile stove when it comes to fuel—efficiently using coal, oil, or wood. This Lanco stove is designed and built to give exceptional service, with convenient drafts and damper for safe control. It can be used anywhere, either installed as a companion to a gas or electric range or used alone. Its firebox is large and deep with duplex grates for wood or coal, and a large tight ashpan in a deep ashpit chamber is furnished for clean and convenient handling. In addition to full-length circulation flues at both sides, the Kitchen Heater has a full return flue at the back, with a scorch shield that continuously radiates heat out rather than absorbing it. Oil-burning equipment for this stove includes a constant-level valve for connection with pump or gravity feed tank.

While it doesn't use oil, Lanco's Granny's Pride does use coal and wood. It's a brand new copy of a very old kitchen stove and is great for stove-top toast, a holiday pumpkin pie, or to thaw out frozen toes in the wintertime.

Another combination wood-and-coal stove is the Record Pioneer, put out by Lanco. This is a cooking and heating range ideally suited for the hunting chalet as well as a handsome addition to a colonial kitchen.

Cooking and baking can be done quickly, while conserving fuel with Lanco's compact model number 27–12. This stove boasts a cast-iron firebox (that can use either coal or wood), grate, stove top, and lids over four cooking holes. It also has adjustable steel legs, a dumping grate, and a removable ash drawer for easy cleaning.

In addition to the stoves used primarily for the preparation of food and to heat individual rooms, there are models that are designed to heat several rooms at a time. The Lanco Americana is a thermostatically controlled unit that is capable of heating four or five rooms. This model has a double wall pipe that reaches to an 8-foot ceiling with optional 24-inch sections that can be added to accommodate higher ceilings. Other optional equipment includes an insulated elbow kit and a blower. The Americana boasts exchanger stack vents, top and side heat emitting louvres, spark-arresting screen, full-width ashpan and a coating of heat resistant flat black enamel. The

doors are solid cast iron, and the fire doors or fireplace screen hangs on brackets at the back of the Americana when not in use.

The Americana, however, is not the largest heating unit available. Model R-76 made by the Shenandoah Manufacturing Company is a wood heater considered adequate to heat four to six rooms. This unit is built box style of heavy black steel with firebrick liners. There is a cast-iron grate, and, like the Americana, it is controlled by a thermostat. Shenandoah also makes several other models, including one with a special grate, which they claim triples the heat output of the fireplace.

Great airtight stoves that allow just enough air to enter the fire chamber to burn wood for as long as sixteen hours on one fueling are the three different size models known as Big Moe, Little Moe, and Tiny Moe—made by All Nighter Stove Works, Inc. Send for their free brochure.

The Alpiner Stove, Mont Blanc, is a very efficient model constructed of boiler-plate (heavy) steel. It is a step-oven design and offers a feature that makes use of two different cooking temperatures simultaneously. The same principal is incorporated in a larger (Matterhorn) and smaller (Chamonix) version of the same stove.

Atlanta's Hunter model is a combination heater and fireplace. If the doors are swung back, it becomes an open fireplace, and when the cast-iron doors are closed, the welded steel body of the stove serves as a radiant heater. The doors are uniquely designed, each with three screw-type draft-control regulators; the two lower ones feed air directly to the burning wood while the upper one provides additional air to consume the volatile gases given off by the fire. This results in the wood holding a fire longer.

The Ardenne is like most box stoves that are available today but is constructed of solid cast iron with a cast-iron interior baffle system (louvres that direct heat in different directions). It has a flat cooking surface overall, an asbestos sealed door, and firebrick lining. Important features offered by this stove are a gauged draft-control adjustment and the option of attaching the flue to either side rather than to the top of the back only, plus a special hook-style door fastener that gives an airtight close. Also, it is one of the stoves that can be purchased either as plain cast iron or with an optional enamel finish.

The Cawley Stove Company makes 100 percent cast-iron stoves for both heating and cooking. All models are airtight and fully baffled for good heat circulation. They burn the wood slowly from front to back by means of a draft-control wheel on the front loading door, operating a draft distribution plate on the rear panel (to give the fuel complete combustion). These parts are machined so that there is a very tight seal.

One big advantage of these stoves is that if a smaller fire is desired, the interior side baffles may be reversed to create a smaller firebox. This feature is more efficient than using lower draft settings in a bigger firebox, as it requires less heat output.

They are convenient stoves, have a good working height, and are easily loaded. The condition of the fire may be viewed through the door window without having to open any part of the stove, and the easily removed apron or "sweep shelf" is ample to catch any spilled ashes. One of the stove's greatest features is the rotating cast-iron flue collar at the rear of the stove, which makes it easy to accept the pipe from the flue at any given angle within a turn of a full circle. And the cast-iron flue collar will withstand much more heat than a standard sheet-metal elbow. The stoves also have adjustable leveling feet that help keep them level on an uneven hearth.

27

The Fargo Heater is a unique type of stove that has a forced-air front, with an automatic thermostat/blower control. (It forces more hot air out of the front of the stove. This is air which would normally go up the chimney or stovepipe.) It is made of heavy-gauge cast iron, and the door may be lifted off and a screen door fitted so that one can enjoy it like a fireplace and view an open flame. With the tight-fitting door in place and the air-intake controls on it adjusted, it is possible to burn a slow fire all night. The top shelf of the stove is flat, but quite small, so it is only suitable for light cooking tasks. It comes with a cast-iron grate and burns both wood and coal.

Both the elegant cookstoves, the Findlay Oval and the Pioneer Lamp & Stove, are versions of the traditional wood ranges, but with eye appeal. Usually one may select certain optional equipment on the stoves such as a backsplash with warming ovens on top or side water heaters or interior firebox coils for circulating hot water. The Findlay Oval is a Canadian-made appliance. It is a cast-iron, brick-lined, nickel-trimmed, porcelain-coated cookstove. Its large firebox of heavy, half-inch thick firebrick offers maximum heat retention and even cooking temperatures. It has a unique hi-lo grate for easily adjusted summer or winter cooking requirements, with four draft controls and three dampers that ensure precise control over the fire. For use during hot weather, there is a Direct Draft Damper to expel excess heat up the chimney.

The porcelain oven has a very large interior, with a two-position rack adjustment. There are six lids on the top surface of the range, and it has an all-copper reservoir (of nearly 8-gallon capacity) that is soldered with lead-free silver to prevent water contamination. Lots of stain-resistant nickel is used on the door panels, oven front, and interior; the splashback and interior and exterior of warming closet are porcelain coated. This decorative stove burns either coal or wood. (The coal grate costs $50 more than the wood-burning model.) The suggested retail price of this range is about $1,500 (plus shipping).

The Frontier Woodstove of ¼- and $5/_{16}$-inch steel plate has the following features:

1. With door closed, and its front-positioned draft caps adjusted, it can hold a fire overnight and can heat a living space.
2. The models come with a fire screen so you can leave the doors open and see the fire.
3. A split-level stove top that gives a 20 or 30 degrees of variable heat makes light cooking tasks possible.

There are optional adjustable warming plates for the stove that could increase the cooking potential. All the Frontier Woodstoves are firebrick lined.

Both Better'n Ben's and the Fisher Stove (sized "Baby Bear," "Papa Bear," and graduating to "Grandpa" and "Grandma" models) are available. They all give a tremendous heat output. The Better'n Ben's stove is particularly useful if you want to use only the chimney of an existing fireplace, installing the heat-producing backsplash to seal off the fireplace opening, allowing the stove itself to radiate out its heat.

The Fisher stoves really give out tremendous heat, and their design of an airtight firebox and interlocking cast-iron door creates an almost foolproof seal. They are welded steel-plate box-type stoves—lined with firebrick—of a unique patented design invented as recently as 1974. Owners of these stoves find that they can reduce the cost of conventionally heating their homes by as much as 25 to 30 percent. These stoves, because of the two-step level top, can be used for long, slow cooking jobs. There is also a small portable surface-top oven available from this company.

Jøtul's cookstove number 380, until recently "out of production," was originally manufactured for ski huts and hunting camps. Now this model reclaims its place as a particular favorite in family rooms and in kitchens. It combines supplementary space heating with stove-top cooking ability. It is essentially a radiant heater with very heavy cast-iron cook plates and top to give off long-lasting heat for cooking tasks. The entire stove is constructed of high-quality cast iron, and the parts are joined with high-temperature cement to provide an airtight firebox. It is front-loaded and can take up to 18-inch logs.

The Kickapoo line of stoves are based on an adaptation of Scandinavian-style baffle designs for greater heat efficiency. This design is comprised of an established air-flow pattern that allows the wood to burn slowly and evenly from front to back in the stoves. These stoves are a com-

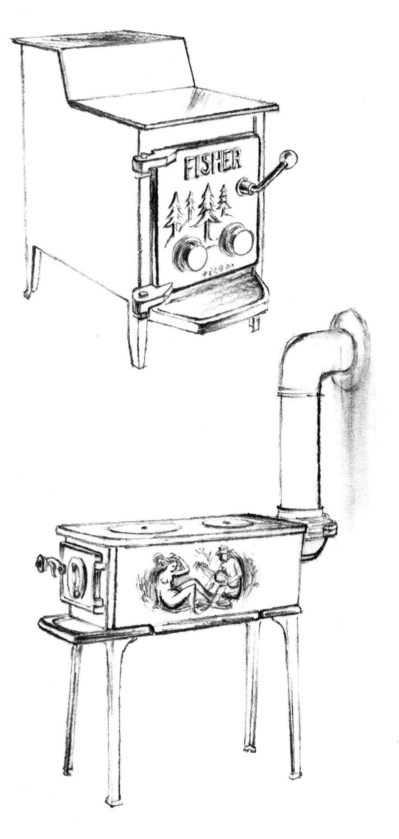

bination of parts of plate steel and cast iron. This company makes stoves for small space heating, for fireplace/stoves, and even a line of home furnaces.

The Pacific Princess by Pioneer Lamp and Stove Company has been the classic of all iron ranges since its appearance in 1911. It now comes with a highly polished top surface and a large built-in griddle-grill with grease trough. Every range has porcelain paneling, but the characteristic nickel trim is an optional feature. Also, you may purchase it with or without a reservoir. The material used in the range is "ductile" iron, a lighter, more porous type of cast iron that cracks with sudden temperature changes and has less ability to retain heat. While the Canadian Findlay Oval retails at a suggested $1,500,

this range, with warming oven and reservoir, lists for about $800.

Le Petite Godin is a particularly attractive little stove that sends out a terrific amount of heat. It is quaint and charming in appearance, with decorative filigree work that imparts a European look to the appliance. But don't be fooled! While it looks froufrou, it is an airtight delight and very functional due to its unique draft regulator, which by a simple turn of the knob can decrease or increase the fire's intensity. There is a small mica window to permit a view of the fire (wood or coal) at all times. There's a swing-aside top that hides a warming surface for a teakettle or small dish. Available in two sizes (small for installing in front of a sealed-off fireplace, and large to be vented into the main flue for house-

size warmth), it is a combination of cast iron and heavy sheet metal. The top, legs, and fire door may be purchased in a choice of colors of enamel or in plain black.

The Vigilante is a traditional Vermont cast-iron stove that, for the practical New Englanders, was useful as a parlor stove as well as a serviceable wood cookstove. While it may be loaded through the two front doors, it has a specially designed smoke chamber that allows for top loading. The hinges inside the top support an uninterrupted cooking surface, yet the design permits lifting out the griddle for easy cleaning. Every stove comes with two built-in folding drying racks that push out of sight when not in use. The door latches are adjustable so that a tight fit is assured over the years, and the built-in heavy metal flue collar at the back of the range is reversible so a top or rear smoke-release can be fitted. The stove also comes equipped with poker, ash shovel, touch-up paint and a spark screen (in case you want to view the fire as a fireplace). The doors are asbestos-gasketed for an airtight fit, and the stove has three separate air channels to distribute preheated air to critical parts of the fire, aiding the fueled stove to hold a fire for fourteen hours or longer.

Better'n Ben's is a woodstove creation that converts a fireplace into a type of home hearth. It claims airtight efficiency, using the Scandinavian front-operated damper principle. It has a nonasbestos gasket and a positive locking device on the door (along with the draft control) to ensure tight closures. There is an adjustable fireplace cover panel (no

stovepipe is needed nor any masonry changes) that can be installed very quickly and which uses the fireplace chimney. The flat top surface can be used for slow-cooking foods (soups and stews). Better'n Ben's is a combination ¼-inch steel-plate construction, with a cast-iron door and firebrick lining.

An accessory for your woodstove flue is a drum oven, suitable for baking bread and cookies as well as heating up TV dinners. Lanco puts out a sootless model with a 28-gauge steel outside body, back door, and breastplate. It is equipped with a reversible pan rack that may be used as a cookie sheet or biscuit pan. Besides being a practical addition to the kitchen, it can also be used in other rooms with the oven door open as a radiator, giving off quite a lot of heat at no additional fuel cost.

Fire-Prevention Tips for Stove Installation

Fire Chief Pitkin has a simple list of helpful hints to remember when installing a wood stove. They are:

- Keep the stove away from passageways to minimize the chance of getting burned by contact.
- Keep the stove away from exits.
- Find a central location with plenty of space around. You should get the greatest distribution of heat this way.
- Do not place stoves in small alcoves or closets. It may look great, but it's a hazard if ventilation is insufficient.
- Maintain the required safety clearances of 18″ to 36″ depending on what degree wall is fire retardant (depends on local fire regulations).
- Try to locate the stove close to a chimney.
- Use an interior chimney if you can. Any heat loss from the chimney will help to keep the house warm. Exterior chimneys are much more apt to condense creosote in the chimney.
- Be sure you have good working room for removing ashes—you do that often.

Reprinted by permission of Energy Communications Press, Manchester, New Hampshire.

How to Buy Used or Old Woodstoves

There are no bargains in either new or used stoves, and ultimately only you will be able to decide which to buy.

Antique woodstoves—if you can find them—are of comparative value to antique great-grandfather's clocks. But most dealers feel that it's too difficult to tell whether or not a stove is actually burned out. Although you may love the filigree work such as nickel-plated skirts and Isinglass doors that make it possible to look into the fire, you must be wary.

1. Primarily, steer away from stoves that have been painted—that's a sure sign that something is very wrong.
2. Carry a flashlight to examine an old stove for cracks and crevices. If you find the side of the firebox is burned out, and seems to be of thinner metal, seek advice.
3. Bolted-on legs are not too critical. It is in the actual firebox, where the grates are, that you must be extremely cautious. But don't be worried if you don't have the right size grate, because that again can be made by an ironmonger or a tinsmith in your neighborhood. Give them the inside measurements of the firebox and give them about an inch leeway. Better yet, bring them the old grate as a pattern. Tell them that you're going to burn wood, or get one of those combination wood-and-coal grates.
4. Be certain all doors and hinges work smoothly and close as tightly as possible. An airtight stove is most efficient.
5. Check the size and position of the firebox; will it accommodate 14- or 16-inch lengths of wood? (Some stoves can be adjusted to

burn both coal and wood.)

6. Do the drafts and dampers (sliding doors and panels) work easily and close completely?

7. What kind of liner is under the firebox? Firebrick or an area for a layer of sand?

8. Can the ash drawer be easily reached and shoveled out for cleaning? Is there an additional or a built-in shaker for the grate? What is the spacing of the grate?

9. What is the condition of the metal? In both new and used ranges, place a lighted flashlight inside the firebox and inside the oven to see how tight the fittings are and whether or not there are any cracks.

10. Also, if there is a built-in coil water line, or a hang-on reservoir, check them out for rust and leakage.

11. Be certain the lids, especially one that may have graduated concentric removable rings, all fit properly. It is always desirable to have a lid-lifter.

12. Do not be talked into buying a built-in door oven thermometer since they are never placed in a position that is practical in a cast-iron stove. It is better to use two separate (inexpensive) oven thermometers. You can position them in different parts of the oven, one at the hottest, back left-rear, and the other hanging from a rack about one-third of the way from the top.

13. Before deciding, check to see if there is a similar model of a new stove available, and how much it would cost. You might be better off with a new stove.

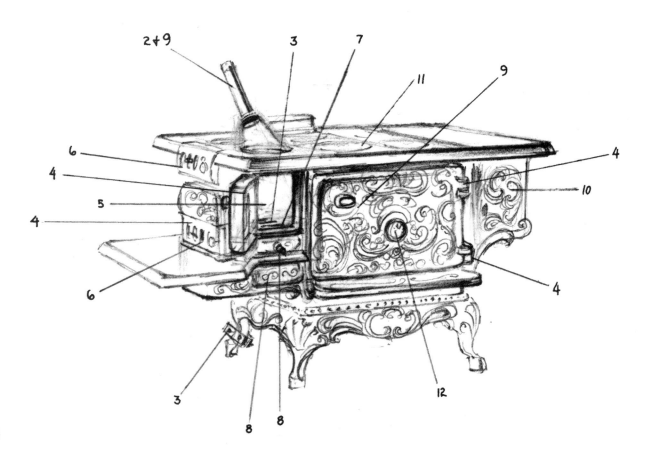

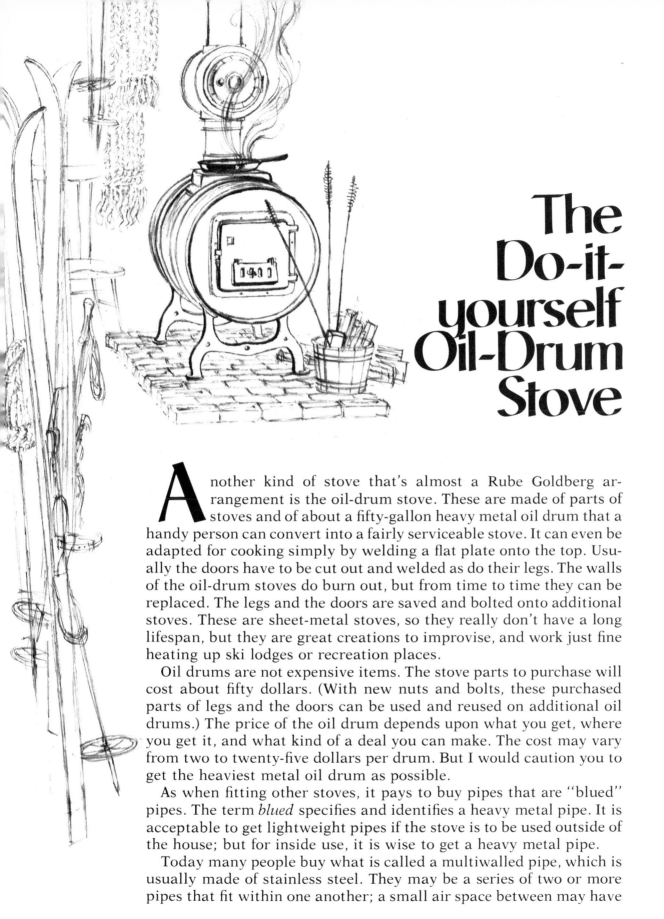

The Do-it-yourself Oil-Drum Stove

Another kind of stove that's almost a Rube Goldberg arrangement is the oil-drum stove. These are made of parts of stoves and of about a fifty-gallon heavy metal oil drum that a handy person can convert into a fairly serviceable stove. It can even be adapted for cooking simply by welding a flat plate onto the top. Usually the doors have to be cut out and welded as do their legs. The walls of the oil-drum stoves do burn out, but from time to time they can be replaced. The legs and the doors are saved and bolted onto additional stoves. These are sheet-metal stoves, so they really don't have a long lifespan, but they are great creations to improvise, and work just fine heating up ski lodges or recreation places.

Oil drums are not expensive items. The stove parts to purchase will cost about fifty dollars. (With new nuts and bolts, these purchased parts of legs and the doors can be used and reused on additional oil drums.) The price of the oil drum depends upon what you get, where you get it, and what kind of a deal you can make. The cost may vary from two to twenty-five dollars per drum. But I would caution you to get the heaviest metal oil drum as possible.

As when fitting other stoves, it pays to buy pipes that are "blued" pipes. The term *blued* specifies and identifies a heavy metal pipe. It is acceptable to get lightweight pipes if the stove is to be used outside of the house; but for inside use, it is wise to get a heavy metal pipe.

Today many people buy what is called a multiwalled pipe, which is usually made of stainless steel. They may be a series of two or more pipes that fit within one another; a small air space between may have insulation material to reduce heat loss through the side walls.

Some people use a combination of blue pipes along with the multi-walled pipe, if it is installed in a wood roof, in the part of the pipe that goes through the roof, or in the part of the pipe that goes from the stove to pass through a wood structure or any part that is flammable. The greatest advantage of these multiwalled pipes is that they are almost fire-retardant. They are expensive but well worth the added investment. For interior installation and particularly for pipes that go through a wood roof or up above the roof (even a foot or more above the roof line itself), I would advise getting multiwalled pipes. A multiwalled "thimble" (a part that goes through a ceiling) is as important to have as the other insulated pieces of metal pipes.

You can get stovepipe circulators that can be fitted into pipes to give off and circulate a lot more heat into the room. This is one of the great uses of that small drum oven (described on page 32) that can be set into the pipe. The warm air circulates when the door of the small drum oven remains open and so a lot of additional heat reaches into a room. They're great, especially for breakfast biscuits or small baking jobs. And they don't cost that much. They're about thirty or forty dollars. It is a good added investment, especially if you don't want to heat up the range oven for just a small baking job.

The Origins of Fireplaces

The need for fireplaces was created by the caveman when he first discovered fire. The fireplace itself took a long time to evolve. In the cave, fire solved many problems for man—cooking better-tasting food, preparing provisions and preserving foods, getting rid of insects, bats, and animals in the cave, and, of course, providing warmth.

The caveman was smart enough to confine his fires in pits surrounded with stones. While he considered fire a precious gift from the gods, he learned to be wary of its dangers when it raged uncontrolled. To get rid of the smoke that burned his eyes and irritated his lungs, he learned to build his fire near a crevice or a hole in the cave, which caused a draft that pulled away the smoke. Indians arranged openings at the tops of wigwams, or poked holes in the roofs of the pueblos, to provide escape for the smoke. Chimneys and flues were wonders of achievement that took centuries to develop.

In colonial days they built walk-in fireplaces, and many of them still exist today. Several stone fireplaces in Pennsylvania, in New England, and also brick fireplaces on Long Island are still functioning since colonial days. Often these fireplaces are the center of the house. In fact, they were often used for structural support!

The big kitchen was the social center for the family. It was the early "family room," and the fireplace made it the only place you could keep warm. Some houses had fireplace openings in the bedrooms. While visiting a friend who lived in a colonial house in Pennsylvania, I was amazed at how a very shallow fireplace in her bedroom put out a large amount of heat with only a few small logs. It drew the smoke up into the throat of that fireplace so efficiently and with no problem! It was not the depth of the firebox that was important; it was the drafting principle. Shallow fireplaces in the bedroom were fairly common in old houses.

Many innovations introduced to the wood-burning stoves as well as fireplaces are rediscoveries of previous advances developed and used in "the-good-old days." Forgotten in changing times, they were "reinvented" repeatedly over the centuries. Some prime examples are the development of the "downdraft principle" (in fireplaces), which involves pulling smoke down behind a false back or core as it travels toward the flue, and the use of oxygen brought in from outdoors to fan the fuel for combustion and to create a draft used to discharge the fire's by-products. A principle practiced for over three hundred years, and still used today, involves the circulation of warm air to create heat, rather than the use of direct radiation.

THE CIRCULATING FIREPLACE

The father of the circulating fireplace is generally considered to be the French physician, Louis Savot. Savot devoted his life to ways of improving health conditions, probably one of the first to apply himself to preventative medicine. In 1579 he built a special fireplace for the Louvre, which had vents near its base to allow air to enter. The air was forced to pass beneath a metal hearth and behind a metal plate to the rear of the fire chamber, where it was heated. The warm air was then circulated through the room by registers placed under the mantel. This is essentially the same method that is used at present by the built-in circulators in fireplaces.

Many early forms of this type of fireplace were doomed to failure, however, because cast iron was a poor material with which to construct ducts and chambers. It tended to warp and crack with direct exposure to the varying of temperature of the open fires, thus allowing smoke to escape into the warm air flow vents. The technique of welding metal plate, a century later, however, solved this problem.

Gauger, another Frenchman, sought to improve the Savot fireplace by combining ventilation with circulation for the first time by using ducts to draw in outside air. This method never gained much popularity, even though the walls of his fireplace were simpler, but the basic idea is still in use today. Gauger realized the importance of constructing a fireplace elliptically to reflect the greatest possible amount of heat back into the room.

THE RUMFORD FIREPLACE

The greatest contributor to the creation of our modern fireplace, however, belongs to one Count Rumford (alias Benjamin Thompson).

In the late 1700s, Count Rumford, working on the problems of smoky

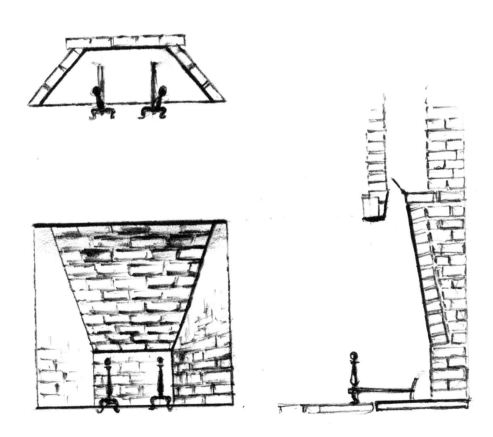

London chimneys, developed a sound and efficient fireplace. His truly scientific study of functioning fireplaces brought about the development of a convection of currents and drafts that made the fireplace almost 90 percent heat efficient instead of the 15 or 30 percent efficiency it formerly had.

The Benjamin Thompson-Count Rumford history is an interesting one. He was a native of Woburn, Massachusetts, and a contemporary of another Ben—Franklin, that is. But because of differences with the colonists at the onset of the Revolutionary War, Thompson-cum-Count Rumford fled to England, where his prominence as an inventor, diplomat, and man of letters was appreciated. He earned the title of count, took the name of his wife's birthplace—Rumford (now Concord, New Hampshire)—and thus the Count Rumford evolution.

Rumford's fireplace design, in 1795, called for a narrower "throat" at the junction where fireplace and chimney connect. The purpose was to prevent excess heat loss caused by too much draft, thus allowing greater heat capacity. The inner walls of his fireplaces were built so that they were wider at the front and slanted back above a shallow hearth, the same feature used in most fireplaces today. Even by today's standards, we recognize the Rumford-style fireplace to be the best.

His work also included designs for furnaces, kilns, and cooking ovens. The modern Dutch oven is believed by some to be one of Rumford's achievements.

His Dutch oven was a heavy cast-iron pot, with a bail handle, and covered by a convex cast-iron lid. It has legs to hold it above the actual hot coals. In Rumford's day it was placed among the hot coals within the fireplace, with an additional layer on the lid, rather than used on top of the stove, or within the oven as it is today. (The results are nearly the same.)

The term *Dutch oven* has been used to describe many and varied metal utensils at different times and in different places throughout history. One recently resurrected version features a separate fire chamber for a charcoal fire that burns under the "oven," or cooking pot, and can be used in either outdoor or indoor fireplace cooking. However, it is not suitable to use in the modern prefabricated fireplaces unless they can support it and have a good draft.

As a surface oven the Dutch oven was advantageous because you did not have to heat up the whole range. A batch of biscuits could be baked over a hot fire, and many foods could be cooked and baked in it. Outdoors it could be buried in a fire pit, covered with coals and dirt, for bean-pot meals or stews, or any one-dish meal requiring long, slow cooking. We often buried it in a fire pit and left it to cook all day, especially when we were camping out or cooking outside at a fishing camp. The cast iron could take the direct heat of the hot embers, with which we surrounded the Dutch oven, after placing the food in it to be cooked. Additional hot embers were put on top and the dirt shoveled over it before leaving it to cook for several hours or all day, providing crock-pot cooked meals, done by wood coals instead of an electric unit.

Know Your Chimneys and Flues

A few years ago I learned a good lesson the hard way. I almost burned down a house that I had newly purchased in the country. It was an old house. I arrived with a friend to spend the weekend there. It was in December of a very cold winter. We built a fire in the fireplace and turned on the small furnace, which also was vented through the same chimney as the fireplace but through a different flue. We retired, thinking the bed the warmest place to be until the house warmed up. In the middle of the night we had a roaring chimney fire.

My friend grabbed an old brass school bell that I had on a chest of drawers and, for a reason never justified, fifty cents in change, which was also on the chest. She ran out of the house and through the woods, vigorously ringing and swinging that bell to alarm people. But there were no people around because the area was isolated. We did have neighbors, each of whom was deaf in one ear and obviously sleeping on their good ears as none came to help. So, the school bell didn't rouse anyone.

Fortunately, the garden hose was still hooked up and I was able to wet down the roof and the basement, where the fire had started, and put out the fire. We never did have to call the fire department. But we really had a scorched ceiling in the basement.

When I remodeled the house, the carpenter I had was on the town's volunteer fire department. It was just a happenstance, but a lucky one. He told us how we could get the fire department to come out and check everything—which is certainly a good tip for any house buyer.

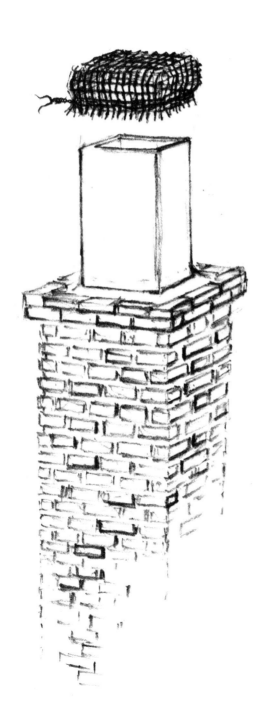

So we called them. With bells clanging, the truck came careening along the dirt road through the woods with volunteer firemen hanging onto it. The firemen dropped chimney-sweep bombs to remove the soot from the chimney flues. We vacated the house, as they suggested. And they spent a great deal of time in the basement.

That was also the year that a poor little raccoon made a nest on the shelf in one of the fireplaces. I had to call a man to come and get the animal. You can guess what happened. Not only did he get the raccoon out of the chimney, but he shot it and took it home. He was a country boy, accustomed to game and hunting, and raccoon meat is good meat. I tell you, I would never go through the tragedy of seeing something like that happen again!

From then on, I always had turkey wire across the tops of chimneys to keep out birds and animals. It's a good sturdy heavy wire—bent, wrapped around, and secured by threading another length of wire. It can be lifted off, removed and replaced, when I have the chimneys cleaned.

A word of safety: If you have just moved into a new or old house with a fireplace and a woodstove, before you use either one, have someone from the local fire department come and check out your chimney. They can spot if there are any leaks in the chimney or other fire hazards. It is mandatory to see if the chimney needs cleaning. Your insurance agent should also be informed of the condition of any fireplaces or woodstoves you plan to use. If he is a thorough agent, he should have them inspected before he approves use of chimneys or fireplaces. (Otherwise he might have to pay up in case of a fire). Most important, they should be tested for drafts and imperfections, poor performance, loose mortar, and all potential fire hazards. Adhere to this routine maintenance of your fireplace at least once a year. The entire system should be checked for any leaks, loose bricks, or stones.

If you're having a new fireplace built, be certain to check the need for a permit and know the specifications to meet standards. Be certain that woodstoves are located in a safe place, i.e., at least eighteen inches or more from the back wall, with heat-retardant material behind the stove against any flammable wall, and more of the same heat-retardant material (bricks, zinc, sand, asbestos matting, etc.) between the stove and the floor.

You no longer have to use asbestos mats. There are zinc under-the-stove mats available now. Sand in a large sandbox is also a good foundation for a cookstove. It's particularly useful because it transmits heat from its surface, thus getting more heat from the stove surface into the room.

When planning to use woodstoves for heat or cooking, you will get your best advice and pertinent information from the guidelines set forth by the National Fire Protection Association. They offer information on fireboxes, working parts, stovepipes, as well as on selection, use, and care.

If you're in an old house, check any unused flues and chimneys. They may still be serviceable. Such a possibility can be checked by your local mason or builder. It is well worth the price, from a safety standpoint. When

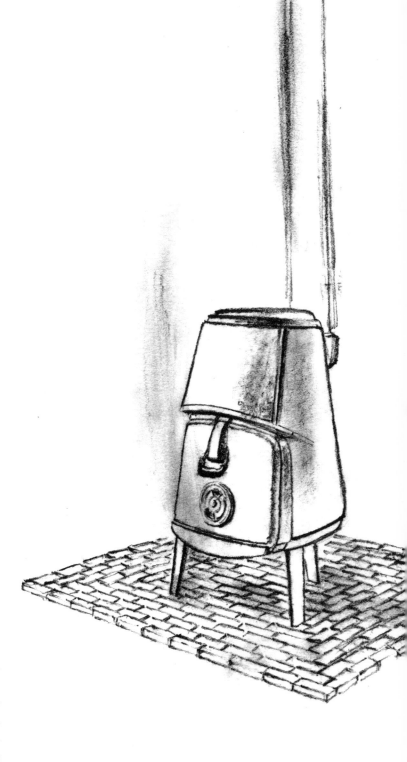

you use the fireplace or woodstove for the first time, you want only the heat and smoke to go up the chimney, not through the whole house!

In many older houses, one brick chimney may often contain several flues piped in from different fire sources within the house. This is a wise arrangement, particularly if it is an interior chimney, as heat radiating from it can warm the whole house.

There should not be a lot of elbows or angles, when venting fireplace flues or stovepipe flues, especially in bricked-up or built-in fireplaces, nor in chimneys of an old house that have not been used in a very long time. It is very important to be sure that all chimneys are in serviceable, sound, and safe condition. Only a brick mason or someone who is used to

working around fireplaces can test and assure you whether or not to use or repair such chimneys. For example, I remember a colonial house that had a shallow bedroom fireplace. There were several brick flues to the chimneys—often in an old house, there is more than one outlet into the chimney flue. They had a way of testing and locating those up in the country. The mason would get on the roof and pour a small portion of fine white sand down the different flues all around the chimney edge. The person below would see whether or not this sand filtered down; it was easily discernable from soot. You knew where there was a workable flue and where some exits were fairly clear.

If you are putting in new flues, other than heat-resistant ceramic

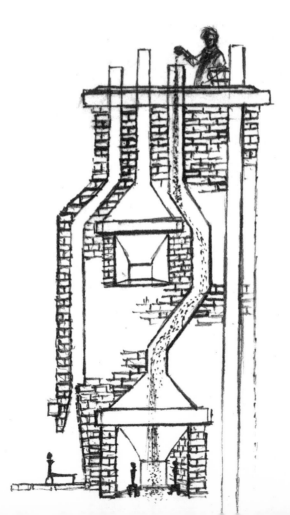

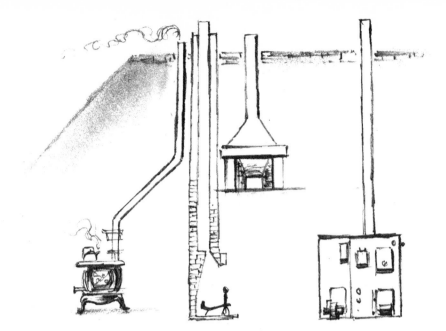

(brick), consider the newer multiwalled insulated steel flues that offer long life expectancy.

Ideally, the best location for a chimney, particularly one with two or more flues, is near the center of the house. However, a single, central flue can have more than one heat-fired source exhausted through it. However, first get the mason or builder to advise you and consult them on the "drafting" and other technical matters. These are decisions best left to the professionals.

Follow these simple guidelines: It is inadvisable to have both a furnace and a fireplace operate off a single flue, since the fireplace requires a greater draft to be serviceable. However, it is possible to tie in a stovepipe into either the furnace or fireplace flue, depending on its placement. (In observing the flues in older houses that have no connection with the furnace, it is likely that the chimney was built for use by wood or coal stoves.)

When the mason is on the premises to check on the number and placement of the chimneys and flues, be sure to have him check their condition, too. You may be able to do a certain amount of this inspection yourself. You'll have to get up on the roof. Then, after tracing how many flues and chimneys you have, observe the condition of the mortar on top (seal) of the flue. Is it *unbroken*, with no possibility of water leakage? Take a screwdriver or pointed piece of steel to probe and poke the mortar between bricks or stones in the chimney. Don't be alarmed if small chunks come out. Even a brick or two breaking loose is insignificant. However, if the mortar or bricks crumble, then they will either have to be "pointed" (remortared) or rebuilt.

Also, if the inside of the chimney near the mouth has become "rotten," it is usually necessary to rebuild the entire top to at least a foot below the level of the roof. Check the metal "flashing" or the overlapping outside shield that surrounds the chimney and runs under several layers or rows of roofing to supply a water seal. From here on in things get rather technical and your best advice can be found in a manual from your library or from bulletins and other expert sources of information. You yourself can do a lot of the care and cleaning of chimneys and stovepipes. There are numerous "how-to" pamphlets and books available.

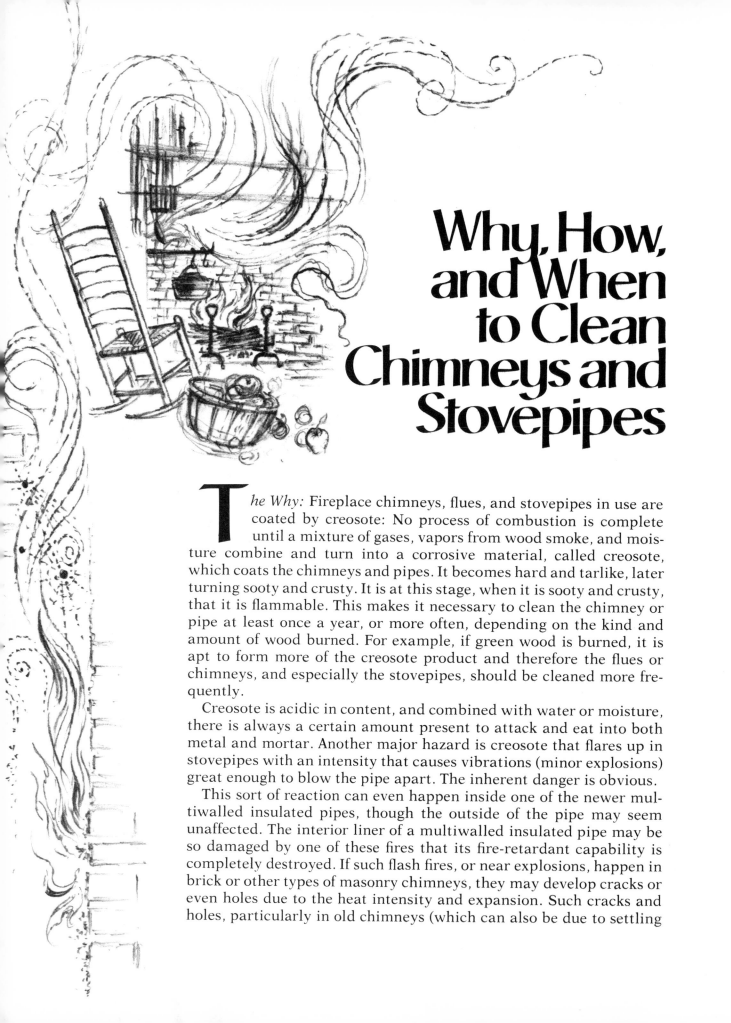

Why, How, and When to Clean Chimneys and Stovepipes

The Why: Fireplace chimneys, flues, and stovepipes in use are coated by creosote: No process of combustion is complete until a mixture of gases, vapors from wood smoke, and moisture combine and turn into a corrosive material, called creosote, which coats the chimneys and pipes. It becomes hard and tarlike, later turning sooty and crusty. It is at this stage, when it is sooty and crusty, that it is flammable. This makes it necessary to clean the chimney or pipe at least once a year, or more often, depending on the kind and amount of wood burned. For example, if green wood is burned, it is apt to form more of the creosote product and therefore the flues or chimneys, and especially the stovepipes, should be cleaned more frequently.

Creosote is acidic in content, and combined with water or moisture, there is always a certain amount present to attack and eat into both metal and mortar. Another major hazard is creosote that flares up in stovepipes with an intensity that causes vibrations (minor explosions) great enough to blow the pipe apart. The inherent danger is obvious.

This sort of reaction can even happen inside one of the newer multiwalled insulated pipes, though the outside of the pipe may seem unaffected. The interior liner of a multiwalled insulated pipe may be so damaged by one of these fires that its fire-retardant capability is completely destroyed. If such flash fires, or near explosions, happen in brick or other types of masonry chimneys, they may develop cracks or even holes due to the heat intensity and expansion. Such cracks and holes, particularly in old chimneys (which can also be due to settling of the building or foundations), can be fire hazards to nearby woods, too, and/or closeby buildings when heat and hot embers escape through them.

If the cost of repairing cracks and holes in an old chimney does not seem feasible, one alternative is to install a stovepipe of sufficient size inside the chimney. Fireplaces should have a smoke-hood set inside the entire firebox. Suspend the whole hood and the stovepipe from the top of the chimney by support wires or rods.

The How: It was not only Santa Claus that came down the chimney at Christmastime! Soon after the Christmas tree was taken down, on the first clear day in January, we tied ropes at the top of the tree and a rope near the bottom. Then one person got on the roof and lowered the rope and the broad end of the tree down the chimney. Someone stationed at the bottom at the fireplace opening grabbed the rope.

At that time an old sheet was fastened over the fireplace opening, and the tree was pulled, by the ropes, up and down in the chimney like a scrub brush to remove all the soot, creosote, and ash accumulation. This one good Christmas-tree cleaning would last us until the spring or the next fall when the fireplace would again be cleaned.

The fireplace chimney was always cleaned twice a year. Another method we used was to tie old tire chains to sturdy ropes and swing them gently from side to side inside the chimney. (This is not the best way, but still effective.) Sometimes several bricks were tied together, a burlap bag wrapped and tied around them, and then, attached to a rope,

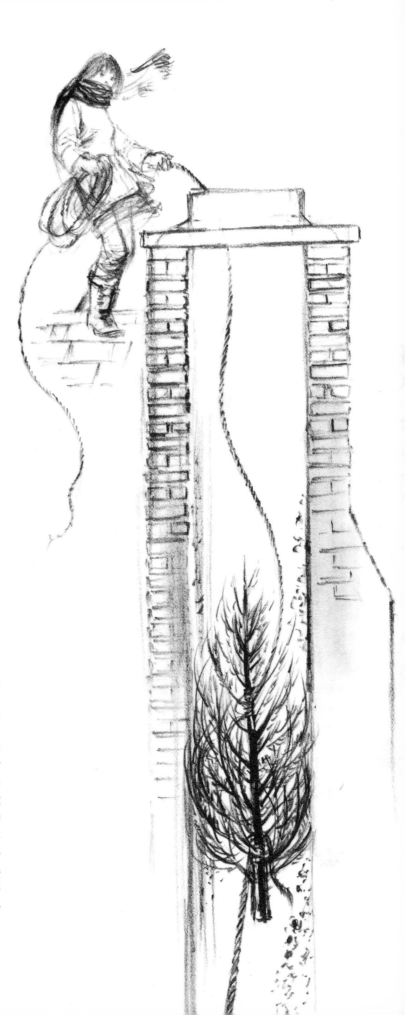

they were gently lowered into the chimney and very gently swung from side to side. We had to do it gently because we did not want to break free any of the mortar. But the Christmas tree scrub brush was always the best. People have used that method for years, and it's a common practice in many sections of the country.

The When: Smoke-filled rooms are not the exclusive turf of politicians. If you don't take care of stovepipes and flues and keep them clean, your rooms will fill with smoke, too.

Clean the stovepipe or chimney when there is a great deal of back draft pouring into the room when you light your fire. A clean chimney or pipe does not smoke—the smoke goes up and out. One of the simplest ways to check whether a fireplace needs cleaning, particularly when a fire has not been built for a few hours or more, is to run your hand along the shelf near the damper and beam a flashlight up into a portion of the chimney to see the amount of soot that is free and loose. If the soot or creosote accumulation is one-quarter inch or more deep, then it is time for cleaning. In the case of a woodstove—and this is really more important because you want peak efficiency from any fires you burn in this appliance—inspect the stove when it is cool or unlighted by detaching the pipe at the flue end (usually an elbow) and see how much deposit is in the entrance. Check as well the pipe coming from the stove and inspect the top of the chimney or stovepipe. If a quarter-inch or more of soot is present, clean!

There are fire extinguishers that look like Roman candles. They can be thrown into the firebox when disassembling stovepipes. They give off smoke that snuffs out any oxygen feeding the fire and thus puts out the fire.

See chapters 17, 18, and 20 for how to build a fire, in both fireplace and woodstove, and when to judge the right time to use for cooking.

Why Do Stoves Smoke?

A smoking stove is due to one or more of the following reasons:

- The ash drawer may be too full, which prevents enough air from getting under the fire.
- The chimney or stovepipe may need cleaning.
- In a new stove the surfaces may be coated with oils that have to be burned off (takes a short time).
- In an old stove it may mean an undiscovered leak that has to be repaired or parts replaced.
- The flue or stovepipe may not be large enough.
- There may be too long a horizontal length of pipe, or it may not be pitched at an angle sufficient to draw or pull the air through. There may be too many bends and elbows in the stovepipe.

Woodstove Maintenance

The primary aim in cleaning is to put on a surface coating that prevents rust formation. Commercial "stove black" can be used, but old-timers used everything from unsalted lard-dipped cloths to their old wax-paper bread wrappers to rub over the stove surface. A light coating of petroleum jelly or any unsalted fat are also good to use as rust inhibitors.

Wadded up newspapers, paper bags, or towels can be used to wipe up excess spatters or spilled cooking grease. Some residue left on the surface can act as a coating and is not harmful. However, if the stove is hot enough for spilled grease to ignite, scoop up some dead ashes and sprinkle over the area to douse the flames. Ashes need only to be brushed away and back into the firebox for easy disposal. Some people keep a box of salt or a bag of flour handy in place of ashes with which to douse out flames. But the salt can corrode the metal, and flour, which has to burn off, makes an unpleasant acrid, scorched odor. Baking soda is also a good fire retardant.

Remember, keep the stove clean, clean, clean! But only clean it when it's cool. Never attempt to clean a hot or warm stove. Chances are that there still may be hot embers in the firebox. This is an invitation to a fire.

You'll need the following cleaning supplies:

- A worklight (the kind used in workshops and garages) or a strong-beamed flashlight (the better to see into corners and crevices, as well as to check for cracks)
- A bayonet-handled wire brush
- An ash or soot rake or a long-handled stiff scraper
- An ash shovel and metal bucket
- A vacuum cleaner with crevice attachment
- Old newspapers (lots!) to catch spills of dirt and soot
- Hammer and block of wood (to cushion and prevent direct hits on metal with the hammer)
- A screwdriver
- Furnace cement
- An adjustable wrench

To remedy a dirty chimney or stovepipe, you need, preferably, a steel brush, shaped either round or square, depending on the shape of the chimney or pipe, and of the same, or nearly the same, interior measurements. The most effective jobs are done by brushes with heavy-duty wire twisted on a heavy-duty spindle of four wires with a sizeable nipple on one end and at least a ¾-inch wire loop at the other end. (This is so you can tie a rope around them and pull them up and down.) Handles for the brushes should be of 7-gauge galvanized wire, twisted and looped for flexibility.

Also very important is to be aware of seemingly simple things such as the stovepipe connection when installing and cleaning the stove. Be certain when the pipes are fitted that the rough or the crimped edge is inside, so that the connection is sealed, because when wood is burned, the

sap and liquid which forms creosote collects, and rolls back into the pipe and into the fire. But with properly

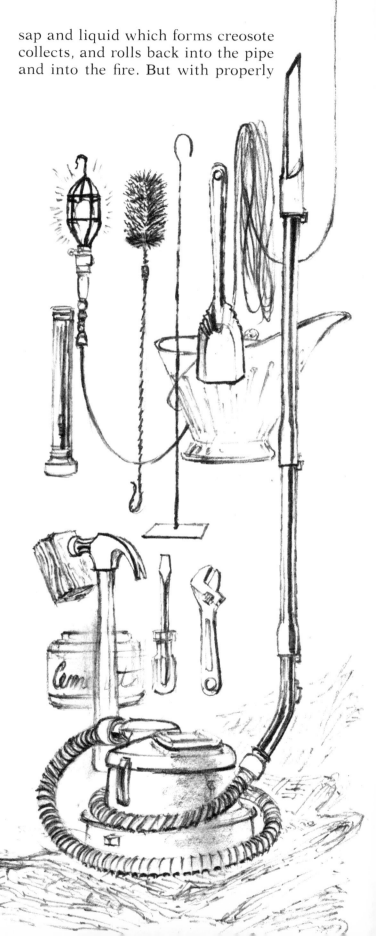

fitted pipes the creosote does not dribble along the outside of the pipe onto the stove or floor.

Remove all parts from the cooking surface and use the wire brush to clean all sides of the parts. Open the side or front of the firebox (depending on where wood is loaded) and shovel out the ashes into the metal bucket. If your stove has an ash drawer, remove its ashes with a shovel. *(Note:* Some stoves may have no grates, in which case there is usually an inch or two of sand layered on the floor of the firebox to act as an insulator between the metal and the fire. If this is so, *do not* remove all of the ashes nor any of the sand, but leave one or two inches of ashes on top of the sand. *Caution:* Do not use "road sand" in the stove, as it may contain salt that will corrode metal.)

Use the work light or flashlight to peer into the interior as you wire-brush and scrape the entire insides of the stove. Scrape out as much soot and debris as you can and then vacuum the insides with the crevice attachment to remove the rest of the soot and dirt.

When my grandmother cleaned the range, she left a little bit of soot scattered on the top of the oven baffle, under the surface lids. She claimed that it kept the tops of the bread or cakes from browning too fast and that it acted as an insulator for the oven. This is a procedure still practiced by many people who believe that the layer of soot on the top of the oven yields more even heat distribution.

There are additional baffle systems (a series of draft controls that direct the heat) in many stoves; these are the ones with the most efficient ovens. Such stoves have one or more series of push-and-pull type of open-and-close control panels. On occasion these are cemented or screwed into place and have to be opened by a gentle tap of a hammer against a block of wood, positioned against the piece of metal to be moved open. *(Caution:* Cast iron is very fragile and can crack if hit directly with a hammer.) Some baffles are screwed or bolted into place and may even be sealed with furnace cement. These have to be unscrewed and the seal tapped free with wood block and hammer. Be certain to scrape off all cement before replacing the sections.

Use the ash or soot rake long-handled brush, and vacuum to clean out all exterior and interior surfaces of the oven. (Some stoves have doors or drawers for access to the surrounding oven areas.)

I repeat: Inspect the entire stove for cracks and corrosion, reapply cement where needed in any small cracks. Then reassemble the stove. *(Note:* If cement is used, wait at least twenty-four hours before starting another fire in the stove.)

More Tips on Cleaning

I f your cookstove has a water reservoir (either the exterior hang-on type or the kind with a circulating coil of metal that carries water to a tank and tap), it will need occasional cleaning (more frequently if the mineral deposits are high). Usually a cleaning two times a year is enough. In a piped-in system, be sure to use a nonacidic, biodegradable cleaner, and follow the package directions implicitly. The small additional cost of a water unit on your cookstove is well worth the money.

The two kinds of water heaters on cookstoves are: the old-fashioned (but still serviceable) metal tank (usually copperlined) which holds about five gallons. This is hinged at the top for dipping into, and hangs off the right-hand side of the stove. Since it has no drain, it is difficult to clean, but the hot water dipped from it can be used to wash dishes or clothes. Do not use it for drinking or cooking.

The other type is the kind that has cold water running through a coil arrangement near the front or behind a cast-iron liner on the left side of the stove, near the firebox. (The coil carrying water is copper.) As the water warms, the rising heat will siphon the water into a tank, with a pipe outlet at the top that carries the hot water out and into a tap at the sink. (*Caution:* It is absolutely necessary to have water flowing through the pipes, particularly the coils in the firebox, otherwise the copper (or liner) will melt and have to be replaced.)

To lessen metal corrosion, it is wise to get a glass-lined tank. For a safety measure, it is also good to invest in a pressure-release valve that lets off steam buildup, preventing the tank from blowing up. Another alternative worth considering is to skip the tank connection and have the heated water from the stove piped directly into the hot water supply of the house. This significantly lowers the electric, gas, or oil costs. (*Note:* A 20-gallon tank attached to the cookstove heats the volume of water almost to the boiling point in about two hours.)

Other parts outside the stove requiring cleaning are the chimney, flue, and the stovepipe. In fact, if the chimney and flue have to be cleaned from the rooftop, do this job first—before you even start cleaning the stove or stovepipe. At least the debris will fall back into the stove, without going into the room or onto the floor.

If it is possible to clean the chimney or flue from inside the house, with the stovepipe from range to wall disassembled, all the better. The simplest way to do this cleaning is to arrange a cloth or a bag over the flue opening and add a series of extension handles to the properly shaped flue brush as you work it; in a scrubbing motion, up and down the entire length of the interior of the chimney or flue. (*Note:* Sometimes you can improvise a suitable flue brush by using a plumber's snake, taped or tied securely to a brush at one end.) Remove the brush and clean out the debris.

One of the easiest ways to determine whether the stove and pipe need cleaning is to remove a section of the stovepipe that goes from the range into the chimney or flue. Inspect the area with a flashlight or work light. See if the buildup of creosote or soot is a quarter of an inch or more. If so, a cleaning is indicated. It is well worth the money to buy steel brushes, rather than plastic

ones, of the proper size and shape to fit the stovepipe and flue. Buy the *round* brushes according to the diameter of the stack or pipe. Buy *square* or *rectangular* brushes according to the measurements of both dimensions.

Use newspapers or a drop cloth on the floor when disassembling the pipe into sections. To aid in reassembling the parts, use a sharp marker, such as a nail to scratch mark the screw-hold points. Leave no more than one bend, or "elbow," in any length of pipe. Otherwise it is too difficult to clean.

Use the brush to remove the creosote and soot from every section. As for the damper(s), some are welded in place and therefore cannot be removed. But they can be held open so you can use the brush to clean out the pipe fairly well. The damper(s) that are removable can be freed merely by reaching inside the pipe to hold the plate, pushing in on the damper handle and twisting it a quarter-turn, which will disengage the handle and shaft. You may have to rock and tilt the shaft a bit to free the handle and

then pull it straight out of the hole. Take care in lining up the spring correctly when replacing the cleaned damper in position. Be sure to check both damper(s) and pipes for excessive corrosion, as they may have to be replaced. Again, buy a good-quality stovepipe; the blue or black heavier metal pipe is worth the extra money, lasts longer, and gives off more heat.

The two simplest ways to keep stovepipes clean is either to add potato peelings to the range firebox or occasionally scatter rock salt on top of the fire. Both of these methods will keep the stovepipe from building up soot and creosote.

About every six weeks, at my grandmother's house, the pipes were disassembled. They were taken outside and put either on newspaper or on the ground on an old sheet kept for that specific purpose. Then the stovepipes were taken apart. The elbows were disassembled, and the damper, on an old spring hinge, was removed. Every part was cleaned thoroughly, scoured, pounded, and rubbed down with a corn-husk brush. (Later we bought her a steel brush.)

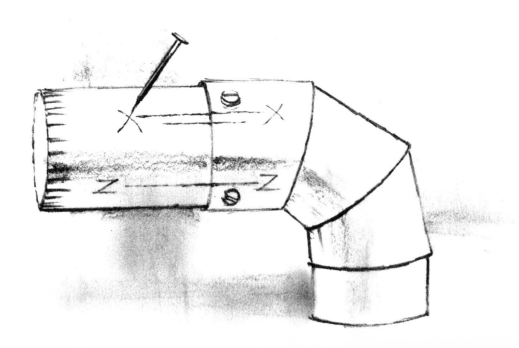

Cleaning the Reservoir Tank

I remember that it was really hard to keep the reservoir clean, especially in our section of the country, where we had mineral deposits in the water. This is how my grandmother handled the problem: She would use a piece of clean sheeting (there always seemed to be an endless supply of muslin, clean sheeting, old sheets) and she would wrap a rock or stone in the sheeting and tie up the whole business with a string long enough so that an end could hang outside the tank. Then she'd lower the rock to the bottom of the reservoir. About every week or so she removed the rock, lifting it out of the tank hand over hand. It was covered with all kinds of mineral deposits!

Sometimes, in order to keep that reservoir water clear, she'd also add some apple cider vinegar. The slight acid of the vinegar not only kept the copper lining shiny, but it also kept the water clear. Often my grandmother would wipe around the top side walls with a piece of vinegar-soaked cloth. When she cleaned the interior of the stove about every four or six weeks, she drained the reservoir and wiped it down.

55

How Wood Burns

For the most efficient use of wood as a fuel in stoves and fireplaces, you should understand how wood burns. Basically, wood consists of cellulose plus a considerable amount of water, like any growing plant. When ignited, the water has to be burned off, and much of the energy in that process is diverted from heating. Therefore, wood that is *seasoned* and nearly dry has greater heat efficiency and is less wasteful. It is more difficult to keep a fire going with green wood because of its high moisture content.

When *banking* a fire, some green wood mixed in with the seasoned wood will hold a fire overnight. A little moisture in the wood is not a bad thing; it makes it last longer. Too much, of course, would put it out, but a little can extend a fire by several hours and keep a stove hot overnight.

Most of our wood-burning lore was handed down to us from the early colonists who learned about our native trees from the Indians. With this valuable knowledge, they soon learned how to have an unlimited wood supply at hand! They learned the value of burning different kinds of woods for different purposes—heat, aroma, flavoring, and preservation of foods, for example. Through trial and error, they soon learned which woods enhanced and which woods spoiled the taste of foods cooked directly over the fires. For example, hickory smoke flavored and preserved certain foods, whereas pine and white birch gave a disagreeable, acrid taste to food. Elm and oak, the hardest and most compact of woods, produced coals and embers that were long lasting—very important when the hearth walls were the only source of heat in the home and the fires held overnight. Our colonial ancestors learned to prolong and regulate the heat with a minimum amount of fuel by banking their fires with a light or heavy coating of ashes—a process still in use today.

We used to bring wood in from the grove near my grandmother's farmhouse, and we did it "Indian-squaw style." My grandmother was not only of French and middle-European extraction, she was one-fourth Indian, and she had learned a lot of Indian lore. We would make branch "skids" for the kindling and logs of wood. To make the "skids" we used a broad branch from a felled tree or a branch that had fallen in a storm, load it with smaller branches and twigs and drag it across the ground—even the snowy ground—as close to the house as feasible. The wood was taken in from there and cut up into sizeable pieces, either for fireplaces or woodstoves.

We did use ashes quite often to control the heat in the woodstove and especially in the fireplace. We would also use wood ashes to snuff out any surface fires or grease spilled on top of the range, sprinkling them over the grease and letting it burn off, then brushing that quickly into the firebox. It was the fastest and easiest way to clean the stove. We preferred to use ashes instead of flour or salt. Salt could cause rust and corrosion on a metal stove, and then it would need polishing. Also, flour gives off a scorched, acrid odor. Ashes absorbed all of the grease while dampening the fire at the same time.

Quite often we did use rock salt. I have a clear picture of my grandmother and my mother scooping out rock salt and putting it on top of the hot embers in the stove to help prevent stovepipe fires. For the same reason, they used potato peelings in the stove. It kept down the creosote—that tarlike substance caused chimney or stovepipe fires. All the potato peelings as well as rock salt went into the hot stove from time to time, to keep down creosote in the stovepipe.

Wood-burning Means Energy Conservation

And it's romantic, too! What can be more intimate than a dinner for two by candlelight, or sitting with someone special by the fireplace after a day of skiing, or the kinship that comes from enjoying good conversation with family and friends around a cheery woodstove or open fire?

If you question how much heat is provided by burning wood as compared to other fuels, here are some statistics: The rule of thumb is that *one* cord of wood is approximately equivalent to each *ton* of coal burned, or to 200 gallons of number-2 fuel oil, or to more than 4000 KWH of electricity. If you want a more realistic approach—review some of your past electric, gas, or oil bills to figure the quantities used, and the jobs done by these fuels, and then translate these figures into how much wood you would have needed. This will give you only an idea, since there are certain jobs that fireplaces and woodstoves are not made to perform. But fireplaces and woodstoves are unequalled when it comes to good cooking, comfortable warmth, and pleasure.

The Right Wood for the Right Fire

According to an anonymous English poet, the rule of thumb for woodsmen goes:

Beechwood fires are bright and clear
If the logs are kept a year.
Chestnut's only good, they say,
If for long 'tis laid away.
But ash new or ash old
Is fit for Queen with Crown of gold.

Birch and fir logs burn too fast,
Blaze up bright and do not last.
It is by the Irish said
Hawthorn bakes the sweetest bread.
Elmwood burns like churchyard mold
E'en the very flames are cold.
But ash green or ash brown
Is fit for Queen with golden Crown.

Poplar gives a bitter smoke,
Fills your eyes and makes you choke.
Applewood will scent your room
With an incense like perfume.
Oaken logs, if dry and old,
Keep away the winter's cold.
But ash wet or ash dry
A King shall warm his slippers by.

59

The kinds of wood suitable for fires vary slightly from one section of the country to another. For ease of care, for long, intense "coaling" properties, and for good burning, the hardwoods, in general, make the best fires. Hickory, for instance, is a wood that packs so much heat power that *one* cord of it is equivalent to two tons of coal!

We used to break up those hickory limbs and put them to one side of the woodbox to be used for baking days. My grandmother used to say, "Hickory is one-hundred percent sure for my bake day." Also, hickory as a flavoring wood is particularly good. The well-known Virginia hams are smokehouse hickory-cured. (Today it is a fairly simple matter to purchase hickory shavings to be scattered on open wood and charcoal fires to season meats and other broiled foods.)

Other hardwoods that are good for fireplace and woodstove use are oak, maple, iron wood, white or yellow birch, beech, walnut, and ash. Cherry and applewoods burn well and give off a pleasant aroma, but their smoke does not give a good flavor to food cooked directly over them. If at the time of cutting a diseased Dutch Elm the bark is stripped from it, and burned to rid it of beetles, the remaining wood is perfectly good as firewood and free of the dangers of transmitting the disease to the woodlot.

Hardwoods available in the West are: manzanite, eucalyptus, madrone, red alder, and tan oak. Softwoods are: redwood, Douglas fir, pine, and spruce.

In the Southwest, Ponderosa pine, oak, and the junipers are used. In Texas, mostly red oak, is used, also some white oak, ash, red maple, beech, birch, elm, sycamore, black willow, and the hickory woods.

There are some "softer" hardwoods that ignite quickly but do not hold the heat for long. These are: aspen, willow, cottonwood, poplar, and basswood.

Softwoods such as pine, fir, spruce, and hemlock make good kindling, but do not retain heat for very long. Ignited, they shoot out sparks, so caution and a fire screen should be used. Because they're filled with "pitch" or "resin," evergreens should be used sparingly since this substance tends to cling inside the chimneys and stovepipes and can be a fire hazard if allowed to build up.

Talking about kindling brings back memories of one of the nicest Christmas gifts I think I ever received. It was a large cardboard box of kindling packets, wrapped and tied with Christmas paper and twine. It included individual packets of pine cones and shavings and bark and wood chips and small twigs; each were wrapped and bundled into just the right size packet to lay in the bottom of the firebox of the woodstove or on the fireplace grate. The woman and her daughter who gave me this gift also taught me everything I know about tying guy ropes on trees that are to be felled. They were as good as lumbermen! But often we would look at trees and not take them down because they were havens for birds, and animals, and homes for squirrels and raccoons. Many a tree was left standing that ordinarily we would have cut. They were true conservationists.

─ How Much Wood? ─

It is estimated that if a stove is used every day of the year for all meals and for all family baking, five and six, and possibly seven cords of kindling and hardwood are needed for the entire year.

Buying Wood

Cut wood takes about six months until it dries out. The drying process can be somewhat speeded up by storing the wood in a sunny place, rigging a plastic cabana or tentlike arrangement above the stack. The plastic transmits the heat and keeps off the rain but still permits air to circulate.

Always specify the kinds, size, and cuts of wood to be delivered.

Be present to oversee (and even help) in stacking it.

Watch out that so-called junk wood is not mixed in, i.e., decayed, diseased, and even very dry-hollow wood, with added softwoods and therefore no bargain.

Specify that you want only seasoned hardwoods; unseasoned wood will not burn easily.

New York is now one of several states in which a standard *cord* of wood is specified and regulated by law. That is, the wood must be compactly stacked within an area 4-feet high by 8-feet long and 4-feet deep, or an area containing 128 cubic feet. Since wood cannot be stacked with no waste space, the more realistic figure is to say it amounts to about 90 cubic feet. Some states permit sales of a *face* cord that measures 4-feet high by 8-feet long, but does not specify depth. It consists of only one row of logs that may be anywhere from 12 inches to 24 inches in length but would only amount to half or less of wood stored in the depth (4 feet) of a standard cord. A *face* cord can also be called a *short* cord, or a *rack*, or a *rick*.

The consumer should be aware of other misleading terms, i.e., "stove cord," (short pieces of wood), "fireplace cord" (long pieces of wood), or a "pick-up cord"—the latter can be nothing more than decayed, hollowed wood, or wood so dry it has no fire power. Also, do not pay by the cord for wood stacked in crisscross fashion by a seller. You will be paying primarily for air space! The volume of solid wood in the stack depends on the compactness and how it is piled. This is why it is wise to watch and even to help stack the wood when it is delivered. (You can, of course, arrange simply to have the pile dumped and do the stacking yourself, which is cheaper since you buy it by the load.)

Sometimes wood is sold by weight. But if you take delivery on newly cut, or "green wood," remember that, when drying, it shrinks and loses weight. So it is wise to request that the seller add another row or two to the cord pile, or that he adds about 20 percent more weight to the load to allow for the shrinkage and weight loss.

STORING WOOD

Storage space for wood is a major consideration, as the firewood needs to be seasoned. Stack the wood on supports at least three inches off the ground. You can raise the woodpile off the ground by using stone or scrapwood supports. Remember that air must circulate to prevent decay and to season (dry) the wood. (For the city dweller it is most practical to use only seasoned wood, as storage space is at a premium.) Pressed wood-pulp logs are now packaged and sold in supermarkets, but these are not recommended as a source of heat for cooking purposes. You get too hot a fire if you use more than one pressed wood-pulp log at a time, and it's very dangerous.

Alternate Sources of Wood

- Some state forests are opened to woodcutters for a small sum or at no cost. Foresters mark the trees to be cut and, after you get permission, you do the cutting and hauling.
- The tops of trees that loggers sometimes leave behind make excellent firewood when cut up.
- Owners of woodlands and foresters are glad to have the tops and limbs cleared from their woods, as they can be a fire hazard in times of dry spells and droughts.
- Woodland owners, in particular those in the Tree Farm Programs, have a need for trees to be thinned out and will usually give you the wood in exchange for your labor. The local or county forester can put you in touch with the people and the programs.
- The town dump as a source of supply may be a big bonanza find.
- Trees in the neighborhood that are cut down to make way for building are good for firewood. So are storm-damaged and deformed trees.
- Contact the nearest Forest Ranger Service, state park officials, and county or state extension services. For no fee or for a small fee, you may be able to cut wood from federal, state or county land, and need only your own labor and a means of transporting the wood from the area.
- Electric power and telephone linemen crews trim limbs and branches often, and they are only too happy to let you take the wood if you do it within two days.
- Road builders and maintenance crews also give permission to cut up and remove the wood within set periods of time.
- Land developers for shopping centers and other construction sites are another possible source.

Healthy, Wholesome Exercise

To keep fit there is no healthier, more wholesome exercise than wood cutting. It gets you out into the fresh air where you can warm up your muscles and reap the benefits of having wood to burn. Cutting your own wood, with respect for a few precautions, is an enjoyable sport that pays off handsomely. It can be more beneficial than lifting barbells and is cheaper than a health-club membership.

If you are inexperienced at felling trees, observe the advice of tree cutters. Don't take chances! If you're a beginner, start with small trees. Get into the practice of walking around the tree to find the side with the heaviest branches; chances are that their weight will cause them to fall in that direction. Also, check to see in which direction a tree naturally leans. If the tree leans and has branches going in the same direction, that is the way it will fall when cut.

Make your cut on the side opposite the leaning and heavy branches. It may have to be guided by ropes to fall in a certain area, especially if there are other trees in the way, or branches from other trees that may "hang up" your tree or cause it to swing in a dangerous manner. If you do have to use ropes as guidelines, try to take up some of the pressure of pulling by tying or winding the rope around the trunk(s) of other trees, letting out the rope gradually to guide the speed and direction of the fall.

Before you do any cutting, clear shrubs and other obstructions away, leaving yourself a getaway route of at least a 45-degree angle from the fall line. Practice a fast retreat before you do any cutting, and repeat it when the tree starts to fall, or when you hear any cracking.

If possible, stay away from cutting trees that grow on an incline, unless you read up on the required technique. It can be dangerous for even an experienced tree cutter to fell trees growing on any incline, because gravity may work against you.

Make the first cut in the direction of the fall, at a comfortable height—about kneehigh, in the shape of a *V* turned sideways. This *V* has its lower side straight into the trunk, about one-third of the way in. Slant your second cut into the depth where it joins the straight cut. This *V* actually makes a sort of hinge for the tree to fall onto when the final cut on the opposite side of the trunk is made.

The final cut is started about one or two inches above the level where the straight-cut notch of the *V* is. Keep cutting until you feel or hear a slight bending away from the saw or axe blade. Don't wait! As soon as the tree bends or you hear sounds, *make a fast getaway and retreat.*

When you're cutting branches off a tree, use the same *V* technique as when cutting down the whole tree. The *V* cut is on the bottom. Then the saw is placed on the top, so that when the branch drops it drops away from the tree, breaking down and away from the saw. Always practice the same precaution of studying the situation, from a safety standpoint, before attempting to cut wood. Cut into the limbs so that the weight of the cut causes the pieces of wood to fall *away* from the saw or axe. Take care that the branches do not swing or fall back on you. And never cut above shoulder height. You can't always predict where the branch will fall; also, it's a great strain on your heart and shoulders.

Deadwood is especially dangerous to cut, because there may be some rotting in the heartwood (center) of the tree, causing the tree to be off-balance. It could, as a result, fall unexpectedly.

A Cardinal Rule for Axe Wielders

After you use an axe, make sure to return it to its resting place. A chopping block with a slit in it to receive the axhead is a good idea. If you know where the axe is, you won't be apt to step on it.

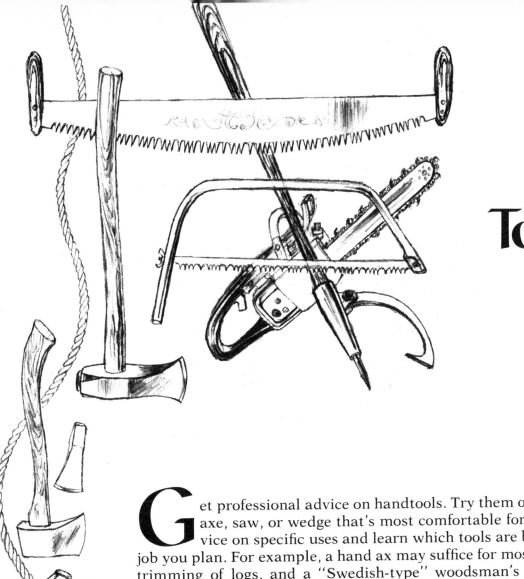

Tools

Get professional advice on handtools. Try them out to find the axe, saw, or wedge that's most comfortable for you. Get advice on specific uses and learn which tools are best to do the job you plan. For example, a hand ax may suffice for most splitting or trimming of logs, and a "Swedish-type" woodsman's saw does an excellent job of cutting up large or small logs. If you use wedges to split your wood, treat yourself to a maul or mallet and spare that axhead when splitting large logs or chunks of wood too big to split with an axe.

If and when you buy a chainsaw, get demonstrations and full information on its use and care requirements. Chainsaws come in different sizes and are equipped to do light or heavy tasks. For example, my editor and her husband team up as family cutters and have a "his" and "her" pair of chainsaws. She cuts small trees with hers; he handles heavier jobs.

Be kind and extend the life of your tools. Maintain them properly to ensure their longevity as well as your safety.

ABRASIVE STONES

Abrasive hand and bench stones are necessary pieces of equipment for keeping tools sharp and in good working order. With a little practice you can learn to achieve the keenest of edges.

Prices of these sharpening stones are relative to the quality. Hard

Arkansas stones, quarried from the quartz deposits in the Ozark mountains, can, when properly used, produce the finest of edges on your cutting tools. These are costly, used mostly by surgeons and wood carvers; it is not necessary to spend money on such fine stone to sharpen axes and adzes. The *soft* Arkansas stones are half the price and adequate for tool sharpening. Also, there is a cheap, natural stone cut from Ohio blue sandstone, known as Queen Creek, that is good.

In addition to these natural stones, Norton Company's Grinding Wheel Division offers a line of synthetic stones made of aluminum oxide under the trade name India, and another of silicon carbide under the name of Crystolon.

A good edge can be made with the use of brown India stones. If speed in sharpening is important, the gray Crystolon stones work well. While they cut faster, they do not produce the finest cutting edge, nor one that lasts as long.

It's advisable that the initial sharpening be done with the synthetic stones and that the final honing be done with the hard or soft Arkansas stones. In this way you get superior edges, with minimal wear and tear on the more costly stones.

To properly "hone" (sharpen) a tool is to work the stone in a circular motion over the edge. This action gives control and keeps the angles of the cutting edge true.

Check whether or not the India or Crystolon stones have been oil-filled at the factory and come ready to use. If not, the stones must be soaked overnight in oil before you use them the first time and may occasionally have to be soaked later.

The best oil to use for this purpose, as well as for lubricating any stone during the honing process, is Bear oil, and Norton Company is a source of supply. Other oils which are acceptable are medicinal mineral oil, Three-In-One oil, and the very light Singer sewing-machine oil. Kerosene can also be used. *Hint:* a good tank for soaking the stones is a discarded icecube tray.

The purpose of the oil, or lubricant on a stone, is that it floats away the metal and abrasive dust that otherwise would become imbedded in the stone and prevent its cutting action. Stones should be cleaned off with a little fresh oil or kerosene before storing them away until the next use.

Wooden paddles, faced with abrasive cloth or paper, are sometimes used as a substitute for sharpening

stones. One side of such paddles may have a coarse grit, and the other side a finer grit that can be used for the finishing honing. Sometimes, emery cloth and fine sandpaper can be used in an emergency, although these must be held taut for proper results. Also, finely grooved machinist files, or other finely grooved files, can be used (infrequently) for a hurry-up job. Files, however, do not do their work by grinding an edge, but by turning up and breaking off a very fine feather of the present cutting edge, thereby creating a new one. As with stones, files should be rubbed by hand over the cutting edge of the axe or adze. Abrasive material drawn over a cutting edge results in uneven cutting angles.

CHAINSAWS AND AXES

If you are really serious about cutting your own wood there is nothing like having what is known as a bucksaw or a two-man saw. If you find one in an ancestor's attic, drag it out for sharpening. But even better is a serviceable but inexpensive Swedish bow saw (unless you can afford to buy and learn to use one of the newer chainsaws).

Swedish bow saws are of good hardened steel, stressed under tension, and have very sharp teeth and blades. They cut through wood with minimal effort and create less sawdust. The versatile bow saw can be used for trimming and pruning as well as for felling trees and for two-man "bucking" in cutting up large logs. To cut trees of twenty or more inches in diameter (rare!), the old two-man buck saw or a heavy duty chainsaw is needed. The bow saw is

relatively inexpensive, stays sharp for a long time, and the cost of blade replacements is small.

Chainsaws require serious maintenance and frequent sharpening to work efficiently. Their expense is justified if you plan to cut at least two cords of wood a year with them. Also, it is imperative that you learn to use them properly and with a healthy respect for the precautions necessary to prevent careless accidents from happening. Since their appearance in the mid-1940s, they have been much improved and made in models from heavy ones to lighter ones, depending on the job to be done. Latest models weigh between 6 and 15 pounds.

Some of the chainsaws today are run on electric current, or recharged by electricity, and are quieter than the gasoline-driven ones. Gasoline saws are less expensive but just as efficient as electric. They are both so noisy that earplugs should be worn when using them. By the way, gasoline saws should operate on unleaded gas, both for the health of their motors—and the country's air!

CHOPPING ACCESSORIES

A "peavey," which looks like the Green Giant's icecube tongs, is a very useful tool. It makes it easier to grip large logs, to logroll, and to secure (with ropes) and dislodge hung-up trees. *Two* peavies make log carrying easier.

Splitting tools are available in all shapes and sizes. One of the handiest and most useful is the good, old Boy-Scout hatchet. But for logs larger than kindling, you'll need a "splitting axe"—one that feels good in your hands and that you can handle well. Practice makes for skill.

A splitting axe is somewhat fatter, with a shorter handle than the one used for felling trees. The head of it will weigh from 6 to 12 pounds, depending on what you can swing easily; on one side it will be blunt, looking something like a sledgehammer. Get one heavy enough to wield, and count on the weight doing most of the cutting, when properly directed. Usually, it's wise to use it with a wedge or two driven into part of the log. You can strike the wedge with the blunt or flat side of the axe, but do not strike it too hard, as the handle may break!

ACCESSORIES TO KEEP NEAR YOUR FIREPLACE OR WOODSTOVE

Lanco's Hudson Bay Cruising Axe can handle most small cutting chores. It is of medium weight, with a balanced steel head on a 24-inch hickory handle. High-grade steel makes the best axes, because they are shaped, heat-treated, and individually tested for proper hardness.

Placement of the Woodbox

The size of your kitchen and how often the stove is used will determine the size and placement of the woodbox. Its location should be as convenient as possible. It may be a box made of wood, or an old clothes boiler or a metal container. If possible, sort and store the wood according to size, kind, and purpose for which it is to be used. Store wood for baking in one section and kindling in another. A two-day supply is usually enough to keep on hand. You do not need an enormous box. It's unwise generally to store wood in the house for much time—insects can and do infest wood, so a protected outside storage area is ideal.

Building the Fireplace Fire

I always argue with a friend of mine who complains that my fireplace is never completely clean. So once and for all I want to say *why* I don't completely clean it out. (Nor does anyone else who knows about fire-building.)

I always leave one or two inches of ashes on the hearth on purpose, because it will keep the "coals" hot and also help in banking a fire for longer periods of time. Ashes are also a good safety factor. You should have cooled-down ashes handy to damp out flaming fires, and this always gives you a supply you can scoop up and toss on a hot burning fire. A bed of ashes in the fireplace also helps ignite the fireplace fire.

However, you do *not* want ashes in cookstoves or woodstoves. Always start a fire in a cleaned out stove. Remove any ashes before starting a fire, because you want as much draft (air) coming from under the fire as possible.

For proper combustion air must circulate around the burning wood. It is therefore necessary to raise the fire off the hearth by using either andirons, log dogs, a grate, or even a few firebricks. The first step is to open the damper, so that the air currents start to draw up the chimney. If the fire has not burned for a day or so, there may be a downdraft (dead air) blocking the smoke from being drawn up and out of the chimney.

STARTING OR "LAYING" THE FIRE

"Lay" your fire by crumpling a few sheets of newspaper and putting them under the andirons or grate. Place kindling on top, and lay two split logs so that they almost touch one another, keeping one very close to the back wall of the fireplace and the other in front of it. On top of these logs add a few more pieces of kindling, and then add a third log to form a pyramid. There will, and should, be some air space between the logs, so that during the igniting there will be more air combustion, and therefore more intense burning. (A properly burning fire gives off a slight sizzle or hissing sound.)

At this point, and before you even touch a light to your fire (especially if there has been no fire burning there for a day), it is advisable to twist or roll a sheet of newspaper, light it, and hold it up high inside the fireplace near the open damper so that its heat and smoke reverse any downdraft in the chimney. This causes the smoke and flames to be drawn up the chimney when you light your fire.

Be careful if you use softwoods, evergreens, or pine kindling to place a firescreen in front of the fireplace to prevent sparks from flying out. Accidents do occur!

When you add more wood, or "stoke" your fire, push the burned logs to the back and feed the new ones in from the front. The hotter the back wall is, the more heat radiates in front of it, and into the room. This makes it easier for the smoke to be drawn up the chimney.

For cooking purposes you may wish to rake some coals out to the front or side area of the hearth, and to cook directly or indirectly over them (e.g., wok cooking). Always keep in mind that pans, if you use them, have to be turned since you not only have heat under them, but radiating around them. Remember that it is always hotter on the side nearer the fire. This fact must also be considered if you are cooking in pots or cauldrons suspended over the fire. It is possible to adjust the heat further by partially closing down the damper when the logs are reduced to coals. Don't forget to open the damper again when you throw on more wood.

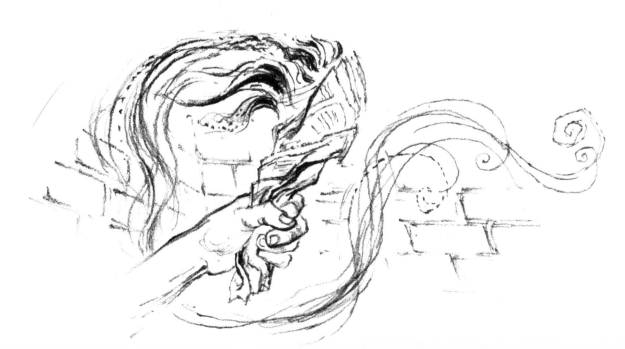

Building the Woodstove Fire

When building a fire in the fireplace, a bed of ashes under the andirons or grate is advisable. It creates better heat distribution. As the embers fall through the grate, they keep their heat. But in a woodstove it is essential to have the ashes cleaned out of the grate and ashbox.

A word of caution: if there are any hot embers remaining, reserve them in a metal container to help start a new fire. If they are to be discarded, be certain to place them together with the ashes in a metal or fire-resistant container. Never empty this container close to the house unless you are certain that no hot embers remain.

Let me tell you about an experience of mine with a supposedly "burned-out" bucket of ashes. I had an outside fish pond and fountain, which was converted in the winter to a compost heap and held a collection of leaves and vegetable peelings. I had just cleaned out my woodstove, placed the burned-out ashes in a metal bucket, and dumped them (as I always did) on top of the compost heap. You can imagine my surprise when, on the following morning, I discovered that the compost heap had been reduced to a pile of black ashes! How close that fire was to the house was scary. Besides, it was a log cabin! I shudder when I think of it.

I now keep two metal buckets to hold leftover ashes. One holds the ashes left to die outside. The other rests near the stove to collect the next supply of ashes. Only the ashes outside remain in the bucket for a full day; I want to be certain they are cold before they're dumped or scattered. (In winter it is helpful to have a supply of ashes to scatter on icy steps or to toss on the snow under car wheels for traction.)

Always start a fire in an ash-free or cleaned-out stove. When starting a fire, open all draft and damper controls. For better "drawing" of smoke and draft up the stovepipe, it is necessary to turn the oven control—usually a sliding door near the pipe and on top of the back of the stove—to the "off" (open) position. Depending on the stove, the fire may be built, and the wood loaded, through a front-door opening or through the top if the plates can be lifted off the firebox section.

Start by crumpling two or three sheets of newspaper and placing them at the bottom of the firebox. Loosely sprinkle a handful or more of "kindling" (small, dry twigs, sticks, bark, cones, or woodshavings) on top. Then, in a crisscross, overlapping fashion, place a row or two of finger-thick "faggots" (larger pieces of softwood dry kindling). Before lighting the fire remember to replace the lids and plate. Light the fire from the bottom *front* of the stove. Wait about five minutes until the fire starts flaming and burning well before adding small "splits" (2- or 3-inch-thick pieces of dry wood). Wait about another five minutes before adding more small "splits" along with some larger (4-inch thick) "splits."

Once the fire gets going well—about five minutes—it is time to half-close the stovepipe dampers. This will retain more heat in the stove, keep the fire burning with less intensity, and make it last for a longer period of time. At this time the heat may be turned on for the oven by closing the oven control (Refer to the section on using your cookstove, page 83.) Open dampers in the stovepipe when adding wood to the fire. Then almost close the dampers. The degree of closing down the dampers depends on how well the fire draws.

After the fire seems to be well underway, add larger splits and chunks of wood to the firebox. The fire will continue to burn unattended for some time, depending on the "coaling" quality (hardness and seasoning) of the wood. If a stove smokes for a few minutes before it catches, don't worry; stoves usually take a while to draw. The dryness or dampness of the day, its stillness or windiness, as well as the wind direction can affect the starting of the fire, so give it about five minutes (if it doesn't drive you out of the house). *Cookstoves should only be used as a supplementary source of heat. Their fireboxes are too small to be used as the main source of heat.*

It's important to get fresh air

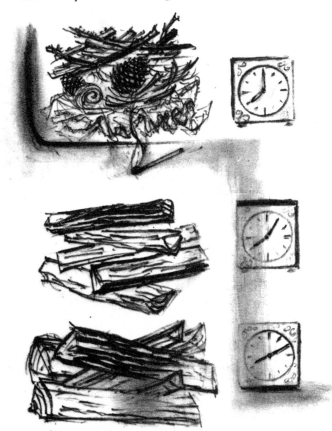

through a closed-up house once a day, especially if you're rebuilding fires. When you have oxygen coming into a house, you get a better fire started and going, one that gives much more heat. Oxygen is consumed by any wood fire, and there must always be a supply of it. With an adequate amount of oxygen you get a much hotter fire, a much faster fire, and one that burns better. Of course, there can be such a thing as getting too much oxygen in a fire. My New Hampshire friends had an overheated stove that got cherry red and cracked because of a fire that burned uncontrolled. (Fortunately, they ended up with only a scorched wall and a no-longer serviceable stove. They use it outside for potted geraniums.)

The cause of that fire—an uncontrolled draft in a chimney flue—has now been remedied by the placement of a "draft cap" at the top of the chimney and additional damper controls in the stovepipe. (A draft cap is a pipe fitted into the chimney opening with a mushroomlike cap that can be swiveled to face into the wind.) My friends not only have a healthy respect for fires now, but they are prepared for any emergency. They have two fire extinguishers, one very near the stove and the phone, and the other one upstairs in case they have to make a fast getaway.

WOODS FOR WOODSTOVES

The kinds of woods to be used in cookstoves are more important to consider than the woods burned in fireplaces, partly due to the small area (firebox) of the stove that provides the heat. Its selection depends on the type of stove and the position of the pans in or on the range, and the duration and the intensity of heat required. For example, you need steady, even heat for baking and roasting; hot heat for top-of-the-stove cooking, such as frying, wok cooking, and boiling; moderate to low or simmering heat for most stews, soups and sauces, or foods that need long and gentle cooking.

For stovetop cooking, birches give off hot flames, great for sautéeing.

Ash gives long-lasting heat that is hot and excellent for wok cooking.

Sugar- and red-maple, beech, wild cherry, and apple woods give moderate heat and are good for baking, roasting, and boiling.

Tips for Humidifying

Woodstoves will dry the air as they heat a room. Did you know that a small amount of humidity in the air makes it even warmer and saves fuel energy? I learned very early about the practical use of the teakettle for putting humidity in the air. The top of that old water reservoir hanging at the side of the range was quite often left off because, again, it permitted humidity to get into the air and warm it.

The Advantages of Wood-fire Cooking

Cooking by wood fire has many plusses. The cook, for one—and an important one at that—is not isolated. Indeed, many assistants are usually available to join in, carrying wood, cutting logs, tending fire.

Special flavors not possible with other kinds of cooking are imparted to foods. Different woods and herbs create exotic flavors.

Fewer pots and pans are required (and the time-honored tools and equipment are not even always necessary). In wood-fire cooking, flexibility and improvisation are a real challenge to the imaginative cook.

Long before barbecue utensils were around, regular cooking utensils were adapted for wood-fire cooking. For example, we adapted two-pronged cooking forks by cutting off the handles and rigging them with thumbscrews. These were placed onto a steel rod for securing roasts, chickens, and foods that we rotisseried in front of a fire. Reflector ovens were built by cutting a one-gallon metal (edible) oil can in half, on the diagonal, and rolling under the cut edges. It was a very simple thing to do with a hacksaw, and we always were sure to place pans under this reflector oven so that they would catch the drippings. Also, we would punch holes at the ends, through which the steel-rod skewer could be secured. Both halves of the can were sometimes used, depending on the amount of food to be served.

Old wooden bread boards or other boards were cut to use for landing decks. They became charred and discolored from use, but that didn't matter. They were great to use under the hot cast-iron pots or any pans. The heat wasn't strong enough to start fires. Also, we had

76

special wooden boards for plank steaks and fish. We were always very careful to put drip pans under the boards. Drip pans can be improvised from folded layers of aluminum foil and crimped edges for depth.

We would get large trays from supply houses on which to organize and line up our ingredients and utensils (as well as to show off and serve the finished foods.) Order is essential in wood-fire cooking!

To handle foods and pans from the fires, hot pads are indispensable, and you should have a good supply of these. I would not suggest using asbestos today, since its relationship to cancer has been discovered. Quilted cotton pads or mitts work quite well, and there are other, more expensive kinds, too, which can be purchased.

You'll really need these mittens for protection, because heat is regulated by moving the pans or food closer or farther away from the source of heat, either directly into or over the embers on top of the stove, or by the reflected heat of oven or fireplace walls. This is similar to cooking on your kitchen gas or electric range, with just a few adjustments in the handling and tending of food. It takes a little more effort than setting an automatic timer, but by following a few simple rules and hints, cooking over embers can become easy, too.

The Right Time for Cooking with Wood

What did we cook where? How did we choose fireplace or cookstove? Often we would use both the woodstove and the fireplace to prepare a certain dish. We would start beef on the woodstove, for instance, to brown it well for stewing in the Dutch oven. Then we'd add the vegetables and hang the Dutch oven (by its bail handle from a swinging crane) in the fireplace, adjusting the distance from the fire by raising or lowering the inside danglehook.

Sometimes we took the iron pancake griddle usually used on the woodstove and placed it in the fireplace over the hot embers. We would rest each side on two firebricks and raise the griddle a little bit above the embers and bake the pancakes there.

In the reflector oven and rotisserie we prepared chicken cooked on a spit, very often legs of lamb and veal, any food that could be skewered and cooked slowly in the fireplace. Anyone sitting near or passing the fireplace reached down automatically to turn the stainless steel rod spit on that reflector oven or on the rotisserie about every five or ten minutes so that the food cooked evenly. We had no mechanical gadgets nor electricity-powered gears to keep it turning.

It is important to have the fireplace designed with the firebox and front area of the hearth large enough to be sectioned off for the purpose of cooking several dishes at one time. Coals can be banked with ease, adjusted, and raked, at the front end of the hearth. In fireplace cooking it is only practice that will help you recognize when the fire or the coals are ready to use in cooking certain dishes. The only other heat control in fireplace cooking is the adjustment of partial closing

and opening the damper in the chimney flue.

If your fireplace does not have an adjustable damper, find out whether the existing damper can be filed or notched so that it can be adjusted. Your local hardware or ironwork shop can help you with this. A damper that can be adjusted will save a lot of heat loss from going up the chimney, instead of into the room or into cooking. It has been estimated that a fireplace without an adjustable damper has 90 percent of its heat lost up the flue!

Fireplaces that have been burning or have stored heat radiating from the firebox walls for a long time actually cook foods best. They also retain a large quantity of hot coals that are formed and banked, which are a source of embers to rake under, in and around, and even over, cook pots and grates.

Cooking by wood fires in the fireplace or cookstove is a challenge to your creativity, flexibility, and especially your ability to improvise. However, the good food that results is worth all the expended effort. Your ability and skill will develop along with your experience. Every fire, every fireplace, and every stove is different in performance, so be patient and practice and get to know all the idiosyncracies. Cooking by these old-fashioned methods requires more pot-watching on your part. The raising and lowering of temperatures is accomplished by moving pots around on or over the heated surfaces or the hot coals.

Cooking time is more irregular in a fireplace or cookstove than when regulated by switches. Best results come from knowing and preparing those foods that are most suitable to this style of cooking. It also helps, when cooking by fireplace, to prepare parts of recipes by your more modern appliances. There is no need to cook the entire dish or meal in the fireplace!

One of the temperamental variances, for example, may occur when baking on either a dry or a damp day, for weather can greatly affect the results. Cakes or bread baked on a dry day usually have greater volume and more tender texture. It may happen that on a damp day the draft being pulled out of the flue or chimney is not as fast moving. Since the air has more moisture, it does not circulate freely or get drawn out as quickly as on a dry day. The fire will therefore not burn as hot because there is not as much oxygen getting to it and the moisture of the wood is not burned off.

The time of day can also affect the cooking. For example, fast hot cooking and sautéeing of surface foods such as pancakes and sausages are best done over the hot early-morning fires in the cookstove.

The season of the year also makes a difference in the cooking because of the different varieties and seasoning of the cut wood available at the time. Remember that most of the energy in wood is used to burn off the moisture if it is to give a hot fire. Remember, too, that every load of wood burns differently because no two loads are alike in kind, mixture, or aging.

The ash, or "coaling," buildup in the firebox or fireplace, and the amount of heat that is given off to radiate around the area greatly affects the kinds of food to be cooked, their degree of doneness, and their cooking time.

Most important is the length of time the fire has been burning in the fireplace or stove. This governs the amount of heat stored, radiated, and generated. How long the heat can be retained determines the kinds of food to be cooked. Adjustments may be made by opening or partly closing dampers or drafts in the fireplace and woodstove, as well as in stovepipes and in the heat panels of the stove's oven controls. All are very important means of regulating the intensity of heat to cook certain dishes. Don't forget that the more efficient use of heat depends on having a clean fireplace or cookstove, including chimneys, flues, and stovepipes.

Fireplace Cooking

Most people are unfortunately unaware that fireplace cooking goes beyond marshmallows, chestnuts, hot dogs, and a dripping wedge of melted cheese. It is really possible to prepare nourishing food in the fireplace—food that is stewed, broiled, roasted and baked, as well as food with uniquely "smokey" aromas.

One thing I'd like to stress is that in starting a fire for cooking, you eliminate the use of synthetic chemicals and petroleum products. They give off noxious odors and can spoil food. They might even be toxic! (How to build and maintain fireplace and cookstove fires is on pages 71–72 and 73–74.) Some people like the visual effect made by adding crystals to color the flames. The use of such products should be avoided since they, too, may be toxic and ruin food. If you want to enjoy them, limit their use to fires for "looking," not cooking!

The best fireplace cooking requires a fire that has been burning for several hours. You should have a good bed of coals or hot embers to work with. A continuous supply of coals that you can move around, under, or over the foods or pans and the radiant or reflected heat off the firebox walls makes all the difference. For example, such foods as baked bread or stews cooked in an iron pot are usually suspended from a crane or chain over the fire and near a heated wall and turned occasionally. Some foods can be roasted or baked in a regular or improvised reflector oven in front of a flaming fire. Actually, every stage of a burning fire may be used advantageously.

The use of heavy-duty (mostly cast iron) cooking utensils is essential. But utensils needn't be expensive. Even heated bricks can be used to cook on. (They're great for broiling fish—one fish on a brick.)

A fireplace fire that's been going for a long time and has a lot of coals is a great spot to place your foil-wrapped packages of foods, such items as potatoes, corn on the cob, or a medley of vegetables. You can dig into the ashes, put the foil-wrapped foods in there, and then lightly cover ashes over them. You will find that you get much more uniform cooking, without having to turn the foods. It's a form of baking in ashes.

Also, the heat of coals can be regulated by covering them with a layer of ashes. This procedure can be useful, for example, if the coals are too hot for placing foil-wrapped potatoes or vegetables directly on them. A layer of ashes scattered over the bare coals prevents the scorching and burning of foil-wrapped food. It also keeps the food from cooking too quickly. This is important for more uniform cooking and especially in baking of breads or cakes or any foods via indirect or insulated heat.

Cookstove Cooking

The surface areas of the cookstove heat differently. Some parts of the surface get very hot and are suitable for frying, sautéing, and wok cooking, whereas other areas have slow enough heats to keep foods simmering or just warm. All degrees of heat for cooking become possible to use when you learn the capabilities of your stove and how to control the heat by adjusting the dampers and drafts in both the stove and in the stovepipes. For example, when my stove has a 2- or 4-inch bed of embers built up in the firebox, I fill the firebox with dry wood (splits or chunks). Then I open the bottom draft just slightly, keeping the oven panel control in the "open" position and the stovepipe damper set at about a quarter-turn. That's when the left front area becomes the hottest. With the lid off, it is the best place to do wok cooking.

Next hottest is the rear left lidded area. I find this the best place to boil foods. The front right area is good for simmering and keeping most foods warm and an excellent place for delicate sauces. *(Note:* if you wish to keep a smaller fire going, or to conserve heat, and do not plan to use the oven, then keep the oven control panel in the "closed" position.)

It is much simpler to build up oven heat in a cast-iron stove than to lower the temperature. To increase the oven heat in a stove that has been burning for long enough to have a good bed of coals or embers, open the oven panel, then the bottom draft under the firebox, and the stovepipe or chimney damper at least halfway. Stir the ashes with a poker until bright embers show, add dry wood of sizable pieces, and let the fire burn hot for about fifteen minutes. Then reload with wood. Check the oven temperature, and when it reaches the desired reading you want, close the draft under the firebox and close the stovepipe damper all the way or almost all the way. (You must have enough pull of air so that the stove does not smoke.) The oven temperature should hold, but if it starts to go down, partly or completely, open both the draft and the stovepipe damper. At this time you may also want to add more firewood.

When you cook in a woodstove, you must recognize that weather will affect your finished food product. For example, you sometimes get bread with a very thick crust if you bake it on a damp, still day. It's very hard to get the oven above 350 degrees Fahrenheit (moderate heat) on such a day. That is one reason why grandmother relied on her hot long-burning hickory wood fire for baking bread and screamed if anyone got near her supply of hickory wood.

It is usually more difficult to cool down a too-hot oven. Opening the oven door is one simple solution. However, this can only be done when roasting meats or other foods where a cool air current does not affect the finished products. Baked goods are more delicate.

The only way to proceed is to close the oven control first. Then open the stovepipe damper so that all the heat goes up the chimney or pipe and completely close the bottom drafts. If possible, throw a large piece of damp wood into the firebox. Some people keep unheated bricks and soapstone handy to place on the bottom deck of the oven. They absorb some of the excess heat.

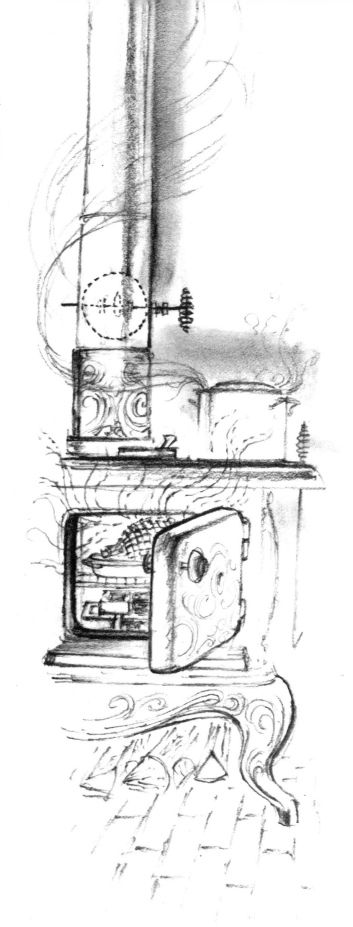

BANKING

"Banking" a stove merely means that you arrange the filled firebox with wood and adjust drafts and dampers so that the fire continues to burn at a slower rate. It is a good idea to keep your fire burning all day. Foods cook slowly over a low fire.

Start with a good bed of embers or coals about 2 to 4 inches in depth. Fill the firebox with good size pieces of dry wood or chunks. Then shut down the stove as tightly as possible—close all drafts and dampers (enough to prevent the stove from smoking), but leave the oven panel in the "open" position. Drafts and damper should only be opened briefly if refueling is necessary.

A well-banked stove can last for seven to eight hours, or overnight, depending on how airtight it is. It is worthwhile to develop an ability to bank well, since building a fire from scratch in a cold stove is a grueling task.

A stove that is too hot can be a fire hazard. It can also get damaged. Surface areas can warp, and some may even crack. To cool down the stove, shut the bottom draft, then open the check draft, close the oven panel draft, tip the lids with the lifter (the cool air flowing *over* the fire holds it down), and open the damper(s) so that heat goes up the chimney or stovepipe.

Rather than adjusting the heat up or down by opening or closing drafts and dampers, it is better to move the pots and pans around over the heated surface to different areas when doing surface cooking. This regulates cooking-heat intensity under the utensils. The ability to judge the varying heat develops with continued use of the stove.

In addition to the hand-passing test that my grandmother used in judging how hot her oven was, from time to time she would also pass her hand over the surface of the range to determine where to place her cooking pots and pans. She had a sensitivity that was developed over a lifetime of cooking.

Tips for Oven Cooking

My grandmother had two kitchen ranges that were almost back to back but in separate rooms. They were vented through a double stovepipe chimney flue. One was called the summer kitchen, which was on the outside of the house. It was used for cooking and for boiling up and washing clothes summertime and wintertime. Because the room was filled with steam most of the time, it was always very cozy and warm.

My grandmother never used a thermometer. In fact, she didn't know that any existed! But she did have certain tests that she used, especially for baking. She used a *hand test,* a *flour test,* and a *paper test.* The paper test I particularly remember, because whenever she used the Dutch oven for baking she would preheat it on the kitchen range, and when she thought it was hot enough she would put on it a very small piece of white rag content paper and then look at it in about five minutes. If it got to be chocolate brown in color, the Dutch oven was right to bake her biscuits or muffins or whatever quick-bread baking she was planning. If it was dark yellow in about five minutes, it was right for breads, cakes, puff-paste pie, or pudding. If the paper was just light yellow in about five minutes, she knew it was fine for a sponge cake or a very light delicate cake. She sometimes used the paper test in a small pan on the middle rack of her range oven.

Most of the time, except when roasting meat or Saturday bakings, she kept the oven door slightly ajar. She felt that it kept the oven dry, let the heat into the room, and also that it prevented it from rusting. When she was ready to use the oven for baking, she would preheat it for at least 30 minutes or more, even on a range that had been fired all day! The oven damper was opened to get air circulating over the top and around and underneath the channel between the oven proper and outside metal surface of the range before it was drawn up into the chimney. Most of the time the oven damper was kept open to allow the heat to come into the room, so that the range oven was partly preheated, making it a simple matter to heat it quickly to proper baking temperatures.

The way she did her flour test was interesting: she placed a small pie pan with about two tablespoons of flour in it on the center rack, about one-third up from the bottom of the oven. If the flour browned in about five minutes—*really* browned—she knew that the oven was ready for any hot baking or biscuit baking.

Her main Saturday baking was planned to start out with a very hot oven. The three or four loaves were placed on the racks, turned and shifted on the racks about every ten minutes because she knew the hot spots in the oven. (Most woodstove ovens, especially in old ranges, have them.) So, for even browning, she had to turn the food around and shift it on the shelves as it baked.

She went from what she called her "hot" baking to her "moderate" baking and her "slow" baking. The breads were baked first, then the pies, and then the cakes. And before the cakes, if we were lucky, the trays of cookies were baked. Three big trays were used.

There was a routine performance: the tray on the middle shelf moved to the top shelf when the second one was loaded and ready. Then second one to top shelf, and third one onto middle shelf; the tray shuffling repeated itself until all cookies were baked.

The slow oven was for very delicate things—sponge cakes, angel food cakes, and meringues.

When I say *hot*, I am speaking of ovens between 400 degrees and 500 degrees Fahrenheit. Breads, pies, and cookies are baked within this range of temperatures.

Moderate I consider to be within the 325 to 375 degree Fahrenheit range, suitable for most cakes and roasting.

A *slow* oven would be within the temperature range of 250 to 325 degrees Fahrenheit.

Grandmother mostly used the hand test. I recall her opening the oven door, placing her hand near the center of the oven, moving it as if waving a magic wand, while counting off the seconds, "one thousand, two thousand, three thousand." If she could leave her hand in for as long as twenty or twenty-five seconds, she considered it a hot oven. If she could stand the heat on her hand for thirty seconds or more, she knew it was a moderate oven. If she could keep her hand in for a minute, she knew it was a slow oven.

These were important tests! A cast-iron stove oven heats up rather rapidly, and it also holds the heat. And you have to be quite certain that you have the right kind of heat that you want if you're doing baking. It's not that important when roasting foods, because you can start with a hot oven, if you want to, which sears the outer surface. (French chefs, in particular, always start to roast poultry in a hot oven, claiming it sets the skin and keeps in the natural juices during roasting.)

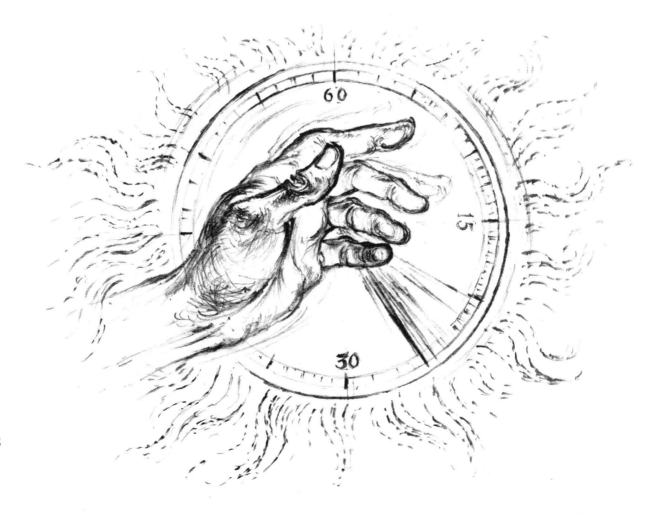

Cooking Utensils

My mother still talks about her sister-in-law coveting all the family pots and pans just as she would any antique in the family collection. She's still fussing about her "gem" pans and waffle irons and what she called the "sad irons," which were actually flatirons with detachable handles. How I would have liked to have had some of those "gems," such as a cooking crane, danglespits, the trivets, the spider, and gem muffin tins and other things to cook with now on my woodstove! Those are the utensils my mother referred to when she complained, "I had all those and your aunt took them." I have no idea where those antique pots and pans are today.

One of the most useful things that I held on to is a 6-quart Dutch oven that I got through the Boy Scouts (not the Girl Scouts!) It has a convex lid, a bail handle and feet, which not many Dutch ovens have. I remember speckled enamelware, gray and white, and the enamelware dipper, which we used to dip water out of the reservoir. We had to be extremely careful with this dipper because it could easily chip. (That enamelware dipper looked so much like the speckled hens that we used to have running around the farm!) It *is* possible to buy the same kind of enamelware today; however, it's not as serviceable as the cast iron. You must use it carefully because it's porcelain (a glasslike enamel on metal).

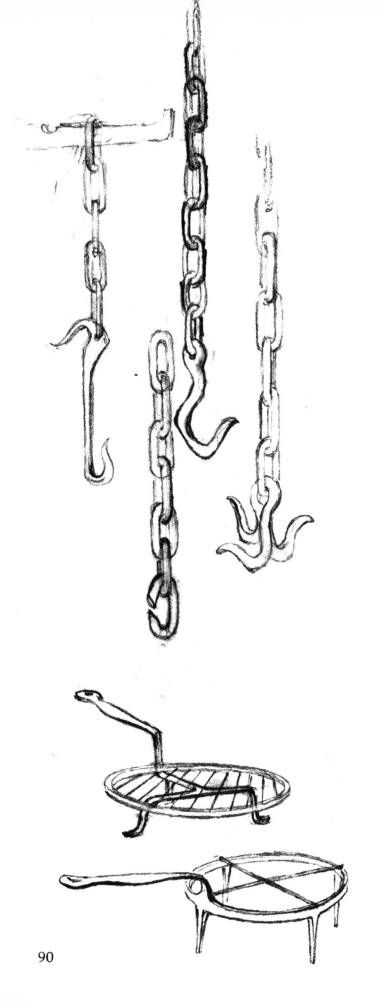

USING THE UTENSILS

When cooking in a fireplace, the best way to adjust and position your pots is with a swinging cooking crane. The distance you want your pans from the fire can be regulated by using *trammels* (which look like large screw-eye hooks) or *danglespits* (a series of chains that you can raise or lower at top or bottom to regulate the distance of the pot from the fire. Cranes, trammels, or adjustable spits can be obtained through your local hardware store, welding shop—or blacksmith! You can improvise trammels by using heavy steel-link chains and cutting a bottom loop to form a hook so that the chain can be raised or lowered.

Metal trivets are indispensable to put under hot pans or between pans and the hot coals during cooking. (Cast-iron "spiders" are skillets with legs and are purposely made this way to keep them an inch or so above the hot coals.)

Cast-iron pots in two or three different sizes are indispensable for cooking and baking. (Avoid plastic handles and covers made of plastic, glass, or light metal, for they melt easily.) The 6-quart size makes an ideal fireplace or woodstove surface oven. Purchase them with indented cast-iron covers and always with steel bail handles so they can be hung over the fire and easily handled.

Pots and pans of heavy enamel-ware are all right for woodstove use but not advisable for fireplaces. Ceramic, terracotta or earthenware do not take sudden temperature changes well and crack over a high heat. They are therefore recommended only for oven use. Soapstone griddles retain heat and are suited for oven or long baking times. But they must be carefully handled since they can crack if dropped. There is usually a metal rim attached to the edge of the griddle and handles for lifting and moving.

Woks should be of heavy metal with nonflammable handles. When using skillets, make sure they come with legs. Skillets without attached legs can be used with trivets, which will keep the pan from being in direct contact with the coals.

Dutch ovens should come with *bail handles* attached (they look like bucket handles), so that they can be used as pots. Ideally, Dutch ovens should be large enough to be used for baking as well as for stews, soups, or boiled foods. Again, select cast-iron material with lids that have an indentation, so that hot coals can be placed on top as well as around the sides and underneath. If possible, it is wise to purchase one with legs, so that the pan itself can then be set slightly above the coals.

Other cast-iron cookware you might consider are bean pots, cornstick pans, "gem" or muffin pans, and partitioned pancake, waffle pans, and griddles. Cast-iron skillets are a must.

One or more grills are valuable utensils. The ones on hibachis are iron and frequently can be used in the regular fireplace or set above the firebox in the stove. *A word of caution:* Be sure that all wooden handles are removed before placing the pot in the fire.

Also, a dual-handled grill, either with a basket arrangement or one that is flat and hinged, is good for

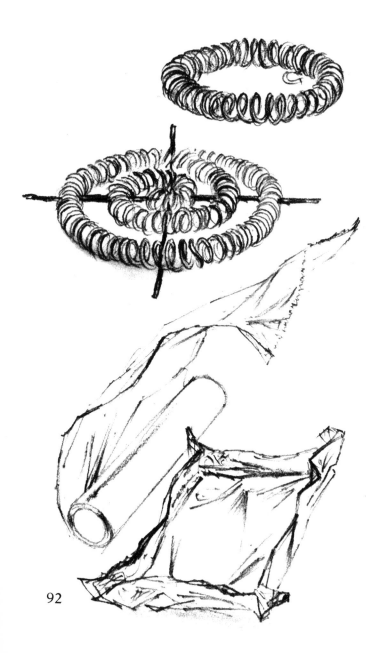

both fireplace and woodstove broiling, either over the firebox hole or in the firebox itself, through a side opening.

You can improvise a small grill that can accommodate grilling fish or a small steak in a cookstove by using a heavy-metal cookie rack over the hole with the lid top removed.

IMPROVISING UTENSILS

If you don't have the dollars to spend for utensils, there are many ways to make them yourself. It's a very simple matter to have long handles placed on regular forks, spatulas, pancake turners, and tongs—all so necessary for woodstove cookery. A visit to your local hardware store or neighborhood handyman can transform utensils you already own.

I've already discussed the making of reflector ovens by cutting old olive oil cans diagonally in half. And you can also improvise with double sheets of aluminum foil and rig it up so that it reflects or bounces the heat off from the fireplace onto the food itself. Soapstone griddles seem expensive when purchased, but with proper care, they'll last you a lifetime. They also save wood because of their excellent properties of heat retention. Snails and coils can be improvised and made of springs that are around the house.

Aluminum foil is great for packing foods to bury in the embers. Double it up and it can be used as a broiler pan. If you're cooking fish in cast iron, and you don't want the flavor to permeate the iron itself, it's a simple matter to line a skillet or cast-iron pan with a double layer of aluminum foil overhanging the edge a bit for easy handling. The fish can be cooked right in the aluminum foil and the mess discarded afterwards. You can also use foil as a reflector over an oven.

Racks (cookie racks and refrigerator racks) can be used directly over the heat (with the lid off the wood ranges for broiling).

You can make rotisserie from long-handled skewers or stainless-steel rods, with thumbscrews and the two-pronged forks to adapt and support them on andirons for use in front of the fireplace.

Broiler baskets can easily be made from parts of the hibachi that have no wooden handles. The iron grates of the hibachi are usually smaller than most grates and can be handled quite simply with long-handled tongs in the fireplace.

With some firebrick you can rig up a small grate that is useful in preparing many, many dishes. The ring that comes with the wok can also be balanced over firebrick and hot embers and the wok itself set into the ring. It keeps the contents from teetering and spilling out while cooking.

I've already discussed how Dutch ovens can be converted for actual baking, especially the 6-quart size.

The log dogs that stand about 4 to 6 inches off the base of the fireplace are also good supports for cookware; they don't always have to be used with a burning log.

If you have a grate in your fireplace, attach two notched rods to the back of the grating for broiling purposes. You can secure a grill or hinged basket to regulate the distance of the food from the fire. For example, when you're cooking

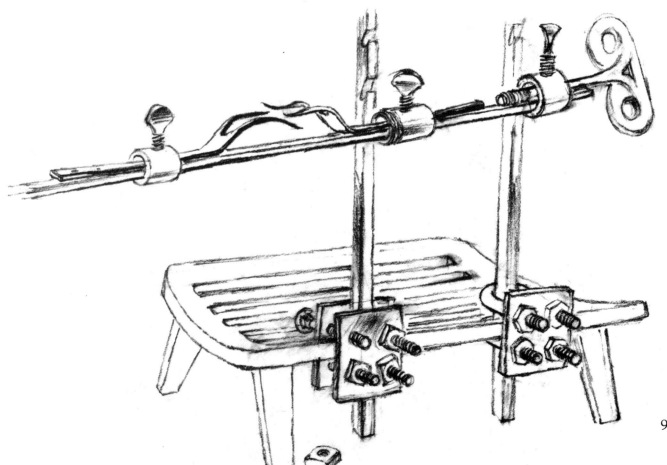

chicken, you cook it very slowly and sear the skin because it's close to the fire. Then you turn it over onto the bone side in the basket and move it 6 to 8 or more inches away from the surface heat, depending on how hot the fire is. Let that second side cook very slowly. You can regulate the distance the food is from the heat source with one of these grate attachments. Fish is cooked farther away from the heat than steaks and other things you might want to sear quickly to seal in the juices.

Iron and other trivets are additional accessories for fireplace and woodstove cooking. They serve the purpose of suspending food in the pan above hot embers and too hot surfaces. Tiles, soapstone, fire bricks, regular bricks, and trivets are all used to absorb the heat and to help you regulate your cooking temperatures. They can also be used as cooking pans, as I've indicated.

In addition, there are planks that can be used for reflected heat cooking. People who make a lot of fish cook them on wooden planks. Tilt the plank at a 45-degree angle, resting it on a drip pan or improvised drip pan of aluminum foil. Heat from the back wall of the fireplace cooks your food. Of course, drip pans are a necessity because you don't want a messy fireplace hearth. I've already indicated ways of cleaning the tops of the ranges and removing grease spots in the event there is spillage and they get dirty.

A roasting spit can be improvised by using a series of clamps and metal pieces to hold a stainless-steel skewerlike fork. It is then rigged up with a set of nonslip smaller tips held firm by thumbscrews to an old set of andirons. Always remember to arrange some kind of drip pan under the roasting spit, and put a reflector baffle in front of the spit, with the curved side facing the fire. This directs the heat onto the food. It is always important to use a hood for roasting or baking in order to take full advantage of all the heat from the fire. A makeshift one, such as aluminum foil, can serve the purpose.

It is wise to have a supply of additional bricks (preferably firebricks) to

hold pans above the raked-out coals or to keep foods warm on the stove by raising them just enough from the too-hot surface. Soapstones and trivets are additional items to consider for this purpose.

You will need skewers, spatulas, tongs, fork and basting brush, all with long handles and of good quality stainless steel for fireplace cooking. Avoid plastic, which the fire would melt.

Also get a supply of large trays and a good cutting board to use near the fireplace or woodstove. Having them will inspire you to get organized and have foods and cooking supplies handy and in order.

We've already discussed how wood ashes cut down fat fires and even put out fires, and how wood ashes can be used to insulate and transmit heat more uniformly (when there is a thin coating). So I'd also like to talk about how wood ashes can be dampened down with kerosene and kept beside a fire. Many people keep a can of a paste-like wood ash-kerosene mixture and spoon a bit on their logs when starting a fire. It also keeps the fire going.

SEASONING CAST IRON

Cast iron can be made serviceable again even if completely rusty. I have a friend who tells me that when he finds an old cast-iron pot or kettle he puts it directly in the fireplace, placing hot coals inside and out until it is red hot. He then removes it and lets it cool before scouring it very well.

When you're seasoning cast iron, reheat it until it's very hot. Then rub the inside and outside with a cloth saturated with unsalted fat or any edible oil (peanut oil, olive oil, etc.). The secret is not to slather on the fat but just to coat it and heat the cast iron in the oven or on the surface.

Repeat that fat-oil treatment inside and outside several times until the metal's pores are filled. Just keep doing that, probably for a half-day. Eventually all you have to do when you clean it is to wipe it out as quickly as possible after it's been used.

Always keep it out of soapy water. Use plain water, then wipe it clean. When you're using cast-iron cookware, *always* be sure that you dry it off immediately. (The simplest way is to put it back on the hot range.)

If you're cooking foods that have an acid content—a beef stew or baked beans with a lot of tomatoes—the cleaning-seasoning process may have to be repeated because acid foods eat into cast iron. You can remove the worst parts of rust with steel wool or a steel brush and then regrease the pan before setting it back in the hot ashes. Repeat the seasoning process over and over and you'll get that black coating inside and outside the cast iron, which is desirable and ideal for cooking. Then the side walls of your Dutch oven or your cooking pans will cook evenly.

It is easier to clean any pan that comes in contact with fire or embers if you soap the bottoms. This procedure isn't necessary to do with cast iron. It is a good idea, however, to apply this to other metal pans—heavy-duty aluminum, steel, or anything with a shiny metal surface. It is not necessary to do this, however, when you are cooking on the surface of the range.

Recipes for Wood-fire Cooking

The recipes I have selected for this book have been especially adapted for use with your wood-burning fireplace or cookstove. I know that the instructions may be somewhat confusing to the cook inexperienced with wood-burning appliances—after all, a woodstove cannot be set for low, medium, or high heat as can the modern range! But you will soon learn, by keeping a close watch on the foods, that you can easily recognize whether or not it is being cooked at the correct temperature. By simply adjusting the pot higher or lower above the fire you can ascertain which setting is suited to the desired temperature.

Cooking over wood conserves energy, utilizing the heat given off by the process both as a method of cooking and as additional warmth to the room. The distinct flavors that develop in foods prepared directly and/or indirectly over embers have no equal in appetite appeal, and the fun of cooking over a wood fire is a pleasure to be enjoyed with family and friends.

A number of the recipes are based on foods served, to speak in metaphor, from the "Boiling Pot" of America—from the days of the Massachusetts Bay Colony, from the cowpokes on the range, from the Conestoga wagon travelers, the Indian adobe ovens, from the Dutch, the Mormons, and the Mexicans, the fishermen, the fur traders, the lumbermen, and the Johnny Appleseeds.

These recipes will, I hope, give you a working knowledge of a variety of cooking techniques to use in fireplace and woodstove cooking. With them as guides, and added experience, you will become as skillful a cook as any trailblazer or pioneer who knew cooking over fire to be a particularly satisfying necessity.

STEAK AU POIVRE

(Serves 6)

The incomparable flavor created by crushed peppercorns burned into beefsteak cuts by panbroiling or direct-heat broiling is a most delicious way to cook this meat. And the wine sauce adds to the flavor. Try some other herb variations instead of the peppercorns, which are also suggested. Try them also on other kinds of meat.

The French frequently still use herbs and twigs of the herbs on their charcoal-broiled foods. They use a lot of rosemary, thyme, and laurel (bay leaves) etc. Thyme is particularly good with pork cooked over an open fire. Rosemary is very good with beef and lamb. Whole leaf or crushed thyme or basil and dillweed are all good with fish.

3½ to 4 pounds steak (sirloin, London broil, shoulder) cut about 1½-inches thick
2 tablespoons peanut or vegetable oil

2 to 3 tablespoons cracked or coarsely ground black pepper
1 teaspoon salt
½ stick butter or margarine
½ cup red or white wine, or brandy

If the edges of the steak are fatty, slash it at about 2-inch intervals so the steak does not curl in direct- or panbroiling. Rub both sides of the steak with the oil. Sprinkle the cracked or coarsely ground pepper onto both sides of the steak and press it into the steak with the heel of your hand. Broil it in a hinged open grill over a very hot-ember fire, cooking it about 5 to 7 minutes on each side (turn only once), depending on desired doneness. Or cook it the same way in a hot, preheated, ungreased 12-inch cast-iron skillet over high heat. Place the steak on a heated platter. Sprinkle it with the salt. In a separate pan (or in the skillet), heat the butter or margarine and add the wine or brandy. Pour the heated wine sauce over the steak and serve immediately.

The same cooking method may be used for interesting flavor variations on steaks as follows:

Especially good for fireplace broiling you may cover both sides of the steak with bay leaves and broil.

Crushed rosemary pressed into the surface of the steak or broiled lamb is an excellent flavor treat.

Also, *crushed thyme or marjoram* may be used the same way.

Note: For each serving allow about ⅓ to ½ pound boneless steak; with some bone, increase the amount to ½ to ¾ pound.

HERBED ROAST LEG OF LAMB

(Serves 8–10)

Here's a roast leg of lamb recipe that can be cookstove oven-roasted or spit-roasted in front of an open fire in a reflector oven. Note also that the marinade basic ingredients can be used to season and help tenderize less expensive cuts of other kinds of meat (chuck, bottom round, flank, pork, etc.).

**1 6 to 8-pound leg of lamb (with
  or without bone)
2 cloves garlic, halved**

Basic Marinade:

**1 teaspoon salt
½ teaspoon ground black
  pepper
1 lemon, juiced
½ cup red-wine vinegar**

**1 teaspoon crumbled rosemary
½ teaspoon crumbled oregano
⅛ teaspoon ground sage
⅓ cup peanut or vegetable oil**

Wipe off the lamb with a damp cloth. Over the top fatty surface of the roast, insert the sharp point of a knife, making four slits about 2-inches deep. Fill each cut with half a garlic clove. Sprinkle and rub the surface of the roast with salt and pepper. In a separate small pan, heat the lemon juice, vinegar, herbs, and oil to the boiling point. Use this mixture to baste the surface of the roast during the cooking time, about every 15 to 30 minutes. If oven roasting, place the meat fat-side up on a rack in a large shallow pan. Cook, uncovered, in a slow oven (325° F.) for 2 to 3 hours, depending on desired doneness, and baste several times with the hot herbed sauce. Or secure the leg of lamb on a spit, being careful to balance it, and spit-roast for about the same length of time, basting it with the herbed sauce about every 10 to 15 minutes. Remove the meat to a serving platter. Drain off all the fat from the pan or drip pan and blend the pan meat juices with any remaining herbed sauce. Add a little water, if necessary, and heat to the boil. Serve the gravy over the hot sliced lamb.

SHISH KEBAB

(Serves 6)

These kebabs can be made with less tender cuts of all kinds of meat.

1½ to 2 pounds less tender cuts of meat, cut into 1½- to 2-inch cubes (lamb for stew, veal breast, pork shoulder, beef chuck, or round)
Basic Marinade (see page 98)
1 clove garlic (surface slashed in several places)
6 medium-small whole onions, peeled and blanched

6 medium-size whole mushrooms, halved
6 fresh, underripe tomatoes, quartered
3 small green peppers, seeded and cut into 2-inch squares
1 medium eggplant, unpeeled and cut into 2-inch chunks (optional)

Trim and discard any excess fat from the meat pieces and place in a bowl; pour the marinade mixture over the meat. Add the slashed clove of garlic (to be discarded at the time of cooking). Cover and refrigerate the meat for about 5 hours or overnight. (If possible, turn the pieces of meat in the marinade once or twice.)

Before broiling the kebabs, partly cook the whole onions in water to cover for about 15 minutes. Cool enough to handle and cut into quarters.

Arrange the meat pieces on skewers, alternating with pieces of onions, mushrooms, tomatoes, green-pepper squares, and eggplant. Cook the kebabs over hot embers about 6 to 8 inches or more above the fire (the kebabs should be slowly cooked and not burned), and baste them with the marinade mixture about every 5 minutes to prevent dryness, for about 20 to 30 minutes. (Cooking time depends on the heat of the fire and the degree of doneness desired.) Serve on a bed of hot cooked rice or on toasted rolls or pita bread.

MARINATED LAMB SHANKS

(Serves 6)

Another variation on a marinade and the technique of giving enough time for tenderizing the refrigerated meat.

3 large (or 6 small) lamb shanks
Marinade:

1 tablespoon salt
5 whole peppercorns
2 bay leaves
½ teaspoon crumbled thyme
½ teaspoon crushed rosemary
¼ teaspoon crumbled oregano
2 teaspoons parsley flakes
1 medium onion, minced

1 clove garlic, minced fine
2 lemons, juiced
¼ cup water
¼ cup red wine vinegar
¼ cup vegetable oil
1 carrot, thinly sliced (optional)
1 rib celery, thinly sliced (optional)

Mix all the ingredients and submerge the meat in the marinade for at least 4 hours (or overnight in a covered dish in the refrigerator). Turn the meat occasionally so that all surfaces absorb the mixture. Drain the meat and cook it on an open grill or in a hinged basket about 6 inches from the embers for about 15 minutes or more on each side.

Note: the marinade may be reserved and refrigerated to use for another meat. It tenderizes less expensive cuts of meat. It will keep for several days if held in the refrigerator.

HERBED HAMBURGER PIE

(Serves 6)

This is a slight variation of the Hamburger Upside-Down Pie, on page 101.

1½ pounds ground lean beef
1 tablespoon butter or margarine
¼ cup all-purpose flour
1 cup diced potatoes
1 cup sliced carrots
1 cup onion rings
½ cup diced celery

1 cup beef bouillon
2 teaspoons salt
½ teaspoon thyme leaves
½ teaspoon ground black pepper
1 clove garlic, minced
1 12-ounce package unsweetened corn-muffin mix

Brown the meat in the butter or margarine. Blend in the flour. Add the ingredients from vegetables through salt. Cover and simmer 5 to 10 minutes. Remove from the heat and add the thyme, ground pepper, and minced garlic. Place the mixture in a shallow casserole dish. Prepare the corn-muffin batter according to package directions. Spoon or spread it over the meat. Bake in a preheated moderate (375° F.) oven about 40 minutes or until the top is browned. Serve hot.

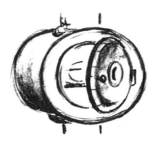

HAMBURGER UPSIDE-DOWN PIE

(Serves 6)

While this simple ground-meat oven-cooked dish is virtually a household basic, it is a recipe that can be adapted to being partially cooked in a skillet over an open fire or on the surface of a cookstove. The biscuit or corn-muffin topping can be baked by tilting the pan to cook from the reflected heat of the hot fireplace or in a fast preheated oven from a hot fire. The little drum oven set into the stovepipe is an ideal place to bake this dish at the time when the biscuit dough or muffin mix is added.

1 small onion, minced	2 tablespoons ketchup
½ green pepper, chopped	1 teaspoon chili powder
2 tablespoons vegetable oil	1 teaspoon salt
1 pound ground beef, broken into small pieces	¼ teaspoon ground black pepper
1 8-ounce can tomato sauce	1 recipe biscuit dough or 1 package corn-muffin mix

In a large skillet cook the onion and pepper in oil until soft and lightly browned. Add the meat and thoroughly brown it. Add the tomato sauce, ketchup, chili powder, salt, and pepper. Shape the biscuit dough (or pour the corn-muffin mix batter made according to package directions) to fit the top of the pan. Place the biscuit or muffin mixture on top of the meat mixture and bake in a hot (400° F.) preheated oven for 25 minutes or until lightly browned.

Invert a large serving platter on top of the dish and turn the two dishes over so that the top of the hamburger dish becomes the bottom, with a corn bread or biscuit base. Serve hot.

TOSTADAS WITH MEAT SAUCE

(Serves 6)

This is an easy, festive dish that can be skillet or Dutch-oven cooked over an open fire or on the surface area of the woodstove range.

1 pound ground chuck or ground round steak	½ teaspoon oregano leaves
1 tablespoon olive or vegetable oil	¼ teaspoon ground black pepper
1 8-ounce can tomato sauce	6 tortillas, or 6 slices toast
¼ cup minced onion	2 to 3 tablespoons peanut or vegetable oil
1 garlic clove, minced	1 cup shredded Monterey Jack or sharp Cheddar cheese
1 teaspoon salt	½ head lettuce, finely shredded
2 teaspoons chili powder	

In a skillet heat the oil and break the ground chuck or round into it. Stir and brown the meat. Add the tomato sauce, onion, garlic, salt, chili powder, oregano, black pepper, and continue to stir and cook the mixture on simmer or low heat for about 20 minutes to blend the flavors. To serve, spoon the hot mixture over the tortillas or toast slices, each lightly coated with olive or salad oil. Top with the shredded cheese and serve each portion on a bed of shredded lettuce.

SAUSAGE AND FRIED APPLES

(Serves 6)

Here's the method my grandmother used when making this delicious dish for breakfast. Sometimes this became a supper dish, served with homemade light, fluffy waffles, which took a little more time to mix and bake than breakfast pancakes.

1 to 1½ pounds breakfast sausage links	½ cup butter or margarine
3 large tart apples, peeled, cored, and sliced	2 to 3 tablespoons brown sugar
	½ to 1 teaspoon cinnamon
	freshly grated nutmeg (optional)

Cook the sausages in a large skillet over moderate heat, turning them to brown evenly, and cook through, about 15 minutes. As the sausages cook, peel, core, and slice the apples. Remove the cooked sausages from the skillet onto a warm platter for holding (pouring off the pan fat) and heat the butter or margarine in the skillet. Try to spread the apples in the large skillet to form one layer. Blend the sugar and cinnamon before sprinkling it onto the apples. Cook the apples over high heat, stirring and tossing them gently for about 3 minutes. Move the skillet to reduce the heat and cook the apples, without stirring, for about 5 to 7 minutes longer, or until the slices start to caramelize and become slightly brown. If desired, sprinkle with nutmeg at serving time. Serve the sausages and apples from the warm platter.

POLENTA

(Serves 6)

This is a basic Italian-style dish to which seafood (shrimp, scallops, crabmeat), cheese (Cheddar, Swiss), chopped meats such as pork, beef, chicken, and sausages may be added. It is a kind of glamorized cornmeal mush.

1 cup yellow cornmeal
1 teaspoon salt
1 cup cold water
3 cups boiling water
3 tablespoons peanut or vegetable oil
1 medium onion, chopped
6 to 10 medium-sized mushrooms, sliced
1 pound shrimp, cooked, peeled, and deveined
1 or more cups chopped cooked meats
1 6-ounce can tomato sauce
water, as necessary
¼ cup chopped parsley, or 2 tablespoons dried parsley flakes
1 teaspoon crushed oregano
1 teaspoon crushed sweet basil
½ cup grated Parmesan

To cook the cornmeal in a Dutch oven or large pot, combine it with salt and cold water and stir in the boiling water. Continue to stir and cook the mixture as it bubbles for about 15 minutes (add more water if necessary).

To prepare the topping, heat the oil in a skillet or wok and cook the onions until translucent. Add the mushrooms. Cover and cook over medium heat for about 5 minutes. Add the shrimp, meat(s), tomato sauce, and herbs. Heat and cook another 5 to 10 minutes for the seasonings to blend. Either serve the hot cornmeal mush (polenta) into individual dishes or if cooled and sliced, brown the pieces on a lightly oiled griddle or skillet and top with the cooked sauce. Sprinkle the top of each serving with grated cheese.

Note: Rather than spooning it out hot from the Dutch oven or deep kettle, the cornmeal mush may be cooked ahead, poured into a large, shallow pan to be cooled and become firm before slicing into individual servings, and browned in a skillet before topping with the hot polenta mixture.

HUNGARIAN GOULASH

(Serves 6)

Stews are slow-cooking dishes. Here are some basics, to be varied as desired. These may be cooked either on a woodstove or in a bail-handled kettle suspended by a height-adjustable hook (danglehook or trammel) on a swinging crane in a fireplace over the open fire.

¼ cup peanut or vegetable oil
2 pounds lean boneless round
   steak or stew meat cut into
   1½ to 2-inch cubes
3 to 5 medium onions, thinly
   sliced
1 tablespoon salt
1 teaspoon coarse ground black
   pepper

1 tablespoon paprika
⅛ teaspoon cayenne
2 cups water
1 to 2 pounds potatoes, peeled
   and cut into eighths
½ green pepper, chopped

Heat the oil in a Dutch oven, large pot, or deep skillet. Brown the meat cubes in a Dutch oven (or large saucepan or pot.) Add the sliced onions and sauté until lightly brown. Add the seasonings and water. Cover and cook over moderate to low heat, so that dish simmers for about 2 hours, until the meat is almost tender. About 30 to 45 minutes before serving, add the cut-up potatoes to be cooked until fork tender. About 5 minutes before serving, stir in the chopped green pepper. If desired, cooked rice may also be served with the goulash.

JAMBALAYA

(Serves 6)

This may be done over direct heat or in a Dutch oven on the surface of the range, or suspended by a danglehook from a swinging crane in the fireplace, or over hot embers in a wok placed on the range or in the fireplace. It can also be cooked in a tightly covered pan in a moderate oven.

¼ cup peanut or vegetable oil
1 medium onion, chopped
1 garlic clove, minced
2 ribs celery, diced
1½ cups long-grained rice
3 tomatoes, diced, or 1 8-ounce can tomato sauce
3 to 4 cups chicken or beef broth
1½ teaspoons salt
freshly ground black pepper
1 teaspoon crushed thyme

1 tablespoon parsley, chopped
½ teaspoon ground cumin
½ teaspoon chili powder
1 cup diced cooked ham or ¼ pound boiled ham, diced
1 pound shrimp, cooked, peeled, and deveined
1 cup diced cooked chicken (optional)
1 cup diced cooked pork sausage (optional)
1 medium green pepper, diced

Heat the oil in a large, heavy oven dish with cover, or in a Dutch oven, or a large wok or skillet. Cook the onions and garlic until translucent; add the celery and stir in the uncooked rice until it begins to stick to the pan and is slightly brown. Add and stir in the tomatoes (or sauce), 3 cups of the broth and seasonings. Cover and cook for 20 to 30 minutes, or until the rice is nearly tender. Add the ham, shrimp, and optional chicken and sausage. Keep the jambalaya warm until serving—reserving the fourth cup of broth to be added if the mixture seems too dry. About 5 minutes before serving, stir with chopped green pepper. Serve hot.

HEARTY BEEF STEW

(Serves 6)

A typical tasty, tender, juicy dish. Stew should be cooked slowly over low to moderate heat, otherwise the meat becomes toughened by high heat. With moderate heat it becomes tender, juicier, and more flavorful—and there is less shrinkage. Also slow, moderate cooking requires less time wasted watching and cleaning up after cooking.

2 pounds beef-stew meat, cut into 2-inch cubes
¼ cup flour
1 teaspoon salt
7 medium onions, whole
1 clove garlic, minced
1 whole clove
1 teaspoon crushed basil
½ teaspoon crushed marjoram
⅛ teaspoon crushed oregano
5 whole peppercorns
2 teaspoons salt

2 cups (1-pound can) crushed tomatoes
2 to 3 long ribs celery, cut into 1-inch pieces
6 medium-size carrots, peeled and cut into 2-inch chunks
6 medium-size peeled potatoes
1 6-ounce can mushrooms, sliced or stems and pieces (optional)
½ cup cold water
¼ cup flour

Trim the excess fat from the meat and heat it in a Dutch oven or large, heavy 3½- to 4-quart covered casserole. Dredge and coat the meat with the mixture of flour and salt. Remove the pieces of fat from the cooking pan and brown the pieces of meat in the rendered fat trimmed from the meat. Peel the onions and leave them whole. Stud one of the onions with the whole clove. Add the onions, minced garlic, and all the herbs, peppercorns, and salt. Also add the vegetables. Reserve the mushrooms for later. Cover and cook the stew slowly for 2 or more hours. The dish should just simmer and be cooked suspended over a fire, or directly on a moderately hot cooking top. About 30 minutes before serving, add the mushrooms and stir in the smoothly blended cold water-flour mixture. Cover and continue to cook another 20 to 30 minutes.

Note: To make this recipe into a *pot roast*, substitute a 3- or 4-pound pot roast (rump, heel, round, or sirloin tip of beef) for the cut-up beef and brown the roast on all sides in a Dutch oven or heavy pan before roasting. Add about ½ cup of water and cover and simmer for 2 to 2½ hours, or until the meat is almost tender before adding the remaining ingredients to cook another hour, or until the meat is fork tender.

BARBECUED TURKEY ON A SPIT

(Serves 6 to 8)

This barbecue sauce can be used on other meats such as pork roasts and chops, ham steaks, beef, and veal. Barbecued chicken, whole or split (fryers or broilers) can be prepared the same way as this turkey recipe—cooked either on a roasting spit, or in a hinged broiler basket 6 to 8 inches above an ember fire.

1 5- to 6-pound ready-to-cook turkey	2 medium-size onions, quartered
leaves from tops of 1 stalk celery	1 clove garlic, minced
2 ribs celery, chopped	2 tablespoons salt
1 medium-size carrot, quartered	1 cup hot water

Basic Barbecue Sauce:

1 6-ounce can tomato sauce	½ teaspoon ground black pepper
½ cup apple-cider vinegar	½ teaspoon cayenne or chili powder
1 lemon, juiced	¼ cup water
2 tablespoons dark-brown sugar	2 teaspoons dry mustard
1 teaspoon salt	

Rinse the turkey inside and out. Drain and wipe dry. Fill the cavity with the mixture of celery leaves, celery, carrot, onions, and garlic. Close the cavity opening by skewering or stitching with string; pull the skin over the neck opening and skewer it to the back. Insert spit, lengthwise, through the bird, and balance it with the forked thumbscrews for even turning. With strong strings tie the legs together and the wings tightly to the body, securing the bird on the spit.

Dissolve the salt in the hot water to make the basting solution (*see* Note). The barbecue sauce is made of the remaining ingredients, and bringing them to a boil before setting aside for basting use during the last hour of spit roasting. Note that this barbecue sauce may be used on lamb, pork, veal, and chicken dishes as well.

By adjusting the distance of the turkey from the embers, so that it does not cook too fast and become dry, a bird of this size cooks in about 3 hours. During the spit-roasting time, the bird should be basted with salt water whenever it looks dry, or about every 15 minutes. Apply basting with a long-handled brush or a swab made by securely tying a cloth to the end of a stick. The turkey may be roasted in an oven the same way, if desired. But because of the dry heat, it may require more frequent basting.

Note: The salt-water basting treatment prevents poultry from burning, yet permits salt to penetrate and flavor the meat. The barbecue sauce is used only during the last 45 minutes or an hour so that the flavors are retained and do not impart a bitter, burned taste.

VARIATIONS ON SOUTHERN FRIED CHICKEN

(Serves 6)

Southern fried chicken may be prepared in a Dutch oven, in a heavy skillet, or in a pan or casserole in the oven.

1 2½ to 3½ pound cut-up fryer, ready to cook	**1 cup flour**
½ cup peanut or vegetable oil	**1½ teaspoons salt**
	½ teaspoon ground black pepper

One of following optional seasonings to be added to flour:

1 teaspoon poultry seasoning	**1 teaspoon crumbled thyme**
1 teaspoon crumbled rosemary	**1 teaspoon crumbled tarragon**
1½ to 2 teaspoons curry powder	

Cream Gravy:

¼ cup fat in skillet	**2 to 3 cups milk or cream**
¼ cup seasoned flour (from above)	**salt and pepper to taste**

Rinse and wipe off excess water from the chicken pieces. While heating the oil in the cooking utensil, dip and coat the chicken pieces in the mixture of the seasoned flour. Place the coated chicken pieces, skin-side down, to cook in the heated pot. Turn them bone-side down when skin side is nicely browned. Continue to cook the chicken slowly for about 45 minutes, or until tender. Remove the chicken to a warm serving platter. Pour off the excess fat left in the cooking pan. Return ¼ cup to the pan and blend in the seasoned flour. Scrape the pan to release the browned bits. To make the gravy, slowly stir in the cream or milk and cook for about 5 to 7 minutes until the mixture is of desired thickness. Season to taste with salt and pepper and pour over the chicken. Serve while hot.

CHICKEN AND DUMPLINGS

(Serves 6)

Proper dumplings require the "don't-peek" rule. The secret of their success is to drop the dumpling batter on the surface of a boiling hot stew and cover the pot immediately. Cook, covered, exactly 15 minutes, without peeking, and serve immediately.

4 to 5 pound ready-to-cook stewing chicken	2 to 3 ribs and tops celery, cut up
1 tablespoon salt	2 to 3 medium-size onions
4 to 5 whole peppercorns	2 to 3 medium-size carrots, cut up
1 teaspoon poultry seasoning	boiling water to cover

Creamy Chicken Gravy:

¼ cup flour	1 cup milk or cream
½ cup cold water	3 cups seasoned stock

Dumplings:

1½ cups sifted all-purpose flour	½ teaspoon crushed tarragon, or caraway seeds (optional)
1 teaspoon salt	1 cup milk
2 teaspoons double-acting baking powder	

Leave the chicken whole or cut it up into 8 pieces. Put it into a 4- or 6-quart Dutch oven or heavy saucepan. Add the seasonings and vegetables and cover with boiling water. Cook slowly until the chicken is tender, about 2 hours. Remove the chicken from the pan, to be returned after the gravy is made.

Reserve the chicken stock for soup and mince or cut up the cooked vegetables to be returned again to the stock. Strain 3 cups of the stock to be used to make the cream gravy. Over a low heat and in the same cooking utensil, blend the flour and cold water to a smooth paste; slowly stir in the milk or cream and then the 3 cups of strained stock. Continue to cook and stir and return the chicken to the pot. Cover the pot, and when the mixture comes to a slow boil, make the dumplings. Combine and sift together the dry ingredients. (If the herbs are used, lightly toss them through the sifted dry ingredients before adding the liquid.) Gradually stir in the milk until just blended. To facilitate spooning out the dumpling mixture, wet a long-handled spoon with the chicken gravy, drain, and quickly spoon a portion of the dumpling batter to drop into the bubbling gravy. Work quickly and spoon the dumplings into the hot gravy. Cover the pan and cook, *without lifting the lid*, for 15 minutes. Serve at once, placing the cooked dumplings on a hot, deep platter along with the chicken, and pour on the gravy or serve it from a separate bowl.

MEDITERRANEAN CHICKEN

(Serves 4 to 6)

This dish has both appetite and eye appeal and yet is a fairly simple recipe to put together. It is a colorful and festive main course to serve to family and friends.

1 frying chicken, cut up	½ teaspoon crumbled thyme
¼ cup olive oil, or peanut or vegetable oil	¼ teaspoon crumbled oregano
	4 large fresh tomatoes, or No. 2 can whole tomatoes
¼ pound ham, cubed or sliced	3 to 4 ribs celery, coarsely cut
1 clove garlic, peeled and scored	1 small can pitted ripe olives
1 large onion, sliced	1 small can stuffed green olives
¼ pound mushrooms, coarsely chopped, or 1 small can chopped mushrooms	1 tablespoon dried chopped parsley, or 3 tablespoons fresh
1 teaspoon salt	½ green pepper, sliced in thin strips
freshly ground black pepper	1 glass dry white wine (optional)
½ teaspoon curry powder	
½ teaspoon crumbled basil	

In a large skillet or Dutch oven, brown the garlic clove in the hot oil and then discard. Add the chicken parts to the hot oil, browning the skin side first. As the chicken pieces brown, remove them and reserve on a platter or separate dish. Add the onions to the hot fat and cook until they are translucent. If fresh mushrooms are used, cook them also in the hot fat, and remove both the onions and mushrooms to the platter. Place the chicken parts, bone-side down, back into the skillet or Dutch oven. Sprinkle the herbs and salt and pepper over the chicken. Quarter the fresh tomatoes (if using canned, leave them whole) and place them on top of the chicken. Add the celery pieces and the rest of the ingredients, except the green pepper, which gets added as garnish at serving time. Cook, covered, over low heat in the stovetop or over an open fire for 30 to 45 minutes. Serve and, if desired, circle the platter with cooked rice.

Note: 1 cup uncooked rice makes 3 to 4 small servings.

BAKED STUFFED FISH

(Serves 4 to 6)

Firm-fleshed fish, either oil coated or placed in foil, may be cooked in a hinged wire basket, about 6 to 8 inches above the fire or, better yet, buried on top of embers that have had an inch or more of ashes on top before the wrapped fish is placed directly into the coals, covered with more ashes to act as an insulator and baked, undisturbed, for about 45 minutes or an hour.

1 3 to 4 pounds whole fish (blue, sea trout, bass, snapper) cleaned and scaled but leave on head and tail
2 tablespoons peanut or vegetable oil
¼ teaspoon crumbled thyme
¼ teaspoon crumbled basil
¼ teaspoon crumbled oregano
½ teaspoon curry powder, or
1 tablespoon parsley flakes or ¼ cup chopped fresh

1 large onion, thinly sliced
1 clove garlic, minced
1 cup celery, including tops, diced
2 firm tomatoes, sliced, or 1 6-ounce can tomato sauce
½ lemon, with rind, thinly sliced

Have ready a double layer of foil large enough to wrap the fish in. Then rub the surface of the fish with oil to prevent it from sticking. Stuff the fish cavity. Do not be concerned about skewering the opening, as the foil will hold it in place.

Arrange the lemon slices along the top of the fish. Now wrap the fish in the foil. If the fire seems too hot, added insulation during cooking may be supplied by overwrapping the foil package with 2 or more sheets of newspaper, which should be wet, before placing the packaged fish in the ash-covered embers, and covering again with a thin layer of ashes. If the foil-wrapped fish is baked in the cookstove oven, it does not need the newspaper overwrap; but because juices may escape in this case, it should have an improvised or regular drip pan under it. Cook for 45 minutes to an hour.

Note: You can vary this recipe by using a small individual fish per serving, seasoned with the stuffing combination in the same way, then wrapped in foil, and cooked individually for about 30 to 40 minutes.

BASIC FISH CHOWDER

(Serves 6)

This recipe offers a typical procedure for making any kind of fish chowder, and you don't have to limit it to just firm-fleshed fish. Combine it with other seafoods or expand its nutritional value by adding one or more vegetables, such as peas, corn, or tomatoes.

½ pound bacon
2 medium-size onions, chopped
3 to 5 medium-size potatoes, peeled and diced
2 carrots, diced
2 cups water
1 pound fish fillets (any white, firm-fleshed fish) cut into about 1-inch pieces

1 teaspoon crumbled basil
2 cups milk
1 teaspoon salt
freshly ground pepper
paprika

In a Dutch oven or heavy saucepan cook the bacon and remove it to be crumbled and added later. Pour off excess bacon fat, but reserve about ¼ cup and return it to be heated in the utensil. Cook the onions until translucent and add the potatoes, carrots and water. Cover the pan and cook the vegetable mixture for about 10 minutes, or until the vegetables are almost tender. Add the fish and basil to the vegetables and cover and simmer for about 5 minutes. Add the milk, salt and pepper to heat through, but do not boil. Serve the chowder and top each portion with some crumbled bacon and a dusting of paprika.

FISHERMAN'S HASH

(Serves 6)

This is a great fast-cooking supper-type family or party dish to do directly over an ember fire or on top of the woodstove range.

¼ cup peanut or vegetable oil
1 medium-size onion, minced
1½ to 2 cups diced cooked potatoes
1½ teaspoons salt
1 teaspoon crumbled basil
freshly ground black pepper

1 pound white fish (perch fillets, codfish, haddock, turbot)
4 to 6 eggs, beaten
1 teaspoon paprika
½ green pepper, seeded and chopped

In a large, heavy skillet or saucepan heat the oil. Add the onion and diced potatoes to cook until the onion becomes translucent and the potatoes heat through. Sprinkle salt, basil, and pepper and stir in the fish and beaten eggs to cook for about 5 minutes.

Cook without stirring for another 5 minutes or until the hash is set on top and browned on the bottom. Sprinkle paprika and green pepper over the top before folding or rolling omelet fashion onto a warm platter for serving.

Note: You can also vary the recipe by using 1 pound of cooked, shelled, and deveined shrimp; or 1 pound of shelled and cut-up fresh crabmeat or lobster tails. If fresh fish is unavailable, 2 6½-ounce cans of crabmeat, shrimp, or lobster will do.

POACHED SALMON

(Serves 6)

This recipe is for salmon steaks, but the procedure may be used to poach other fish steaks or fillets.

1 10½ ounce can chicken broth	1 teaspoon salt
1 cup water	6 salmon fillets, about 4 ounces
1 teaspoon rosemary	each
½ teaspoon shrimp boil	watercress or chopped parsley,
1 lemon, juiced	to garnish (optional)
½ small onion, thinly sliced	

Sour-Cream-Mustard Sauce:

1 cup sour cream	½ cup mayonnaise
1 tablespoon prepared hot, spicy	1 tablespoon cider vinegar
mustard	½ teaspoon salt

Combine the broth, water, rosemary, shrimp boil (a packaged combination of spices), lemon juice, onion, and salt in a large cast-iron skillet. *But,* line the interior of the skillet with aluminum foil to lessen the fish flavor that would permeate the pan. Heat the mixture to the boil and gently slide in the fillets. Do not let the liquid boil again—and lower the heat to prevent it. Cover the skillet and cook the fish for about 5 minutes. To serve the fish cold, leave it in the broth and chill for 2 to 3 hours. Or drain it from the hot seasoned broth and serve immediately, topped with the sour-cream-mustard sauce. The sauce is made by blending together all the ingredients and spooning it over hot or cold fish servings as desired. Garnish with watercress or chopped parsley.

PLANKED FISH STEAKS

(Serves 6)

To "plank" food, secure it by tying or lashing it criss-cross style with heavy string (wetted down to prevent it from burning). Set the planked food slanted in front of the fire to cook by the reflected heat of the fire. Be sure to rest the bottom of the plank in a drip pan (regular or improvised) to catch any juices running off. Remember, when using planks, sticks, or other pieces of wood for cooking, use only green wood to prevent it from igniting, and peel the bark from it or cut off a small chip to taste a piece of the wood. If it is unpleasant, the food cooked on it will also have a bad taste. In planking food (fish or meats), remember to place a drip pan under the bottom edge to catch juices. Improvise a pan with a double layer of foil and crimp up the edges.

3 or more 2-inch-thick fish steaks (any firm, white fish such as halibut or cod)
½ medium-size onion, finely chopped
1 clove garlic, finely minced
½ teaspoon crumbled thyme
½ teaspoon crumbled basil

1 teaspoon salt, or to taste
¼ teaspoon ground black pepper
¼ cup peanut or vegetable oil
½ lemon, juiced
¼ cup finely chopped fresh parsley
lemon wedges, to garnish, if desired

Place the steaks on well-greased plank(s). Combine the onion, garlic, thyme, basil, salt and pepper in the oil and spoon some of the mixture to coat the steaks. Place the planks in a lined tray, in a preheated, hot oven (300° F), or in front of a hot, open fire at a 45-degree angle (with a drip pan underneath to catch juices) and baste the fish again, at least once during cooking, with the onion-herb seasoned oil. Cook the fish for about 20 to 25 minutes or until it flakes easily when tested with a fork. Sprinkle lemon juice and chopped parsley on the planked fish and serve immediately with lemon wedges.

BASIC SOUP STOCK

(Makes 3 Quarts)

A good basic rule to follow when making soup stock is to use 1 quart of water for every pound of bones.

3 pounds cracked bones (such as veal, chicken, beef and/or "soup bones" sold in market)
3 quarts water
1 teaspoon crumbled thyme
3 whole bay leaves
2 whole cloves
½ cup chopped parsley

1 tablespoon salt
5 black peppercorns
2 to 4 ribs celery, sliced
2 to 4 carrots, sliced
3 medium-size onions, chopped
2 cloves garlic, minced
egg shells (optional)

In a large stockpot or kettle place the bones, water, and remaining ingredients (except the egg shells). Cover and simmer for 6 hours or more. Occasionally foam will form on the surface and should be skimmed off and discarded.

After the simmering, remove and set aside the bones and any large pieces of meat. Let the liquid cool slightly before straining it through a fine sieve into another kettle or soup pot. Cool the strained stock until the fat floats to the top and most of it can be spooned off. Meanwhile, remove the meat from the bones and either cut or shred it into bite-size, fat-free pieces to be added to the strained, defatted stock or set aside to use in hash or meatloaf. To clarify the strained stock, without the meat, bring it to the boiling point and add several cleaned, crushed egg shells. Then let the stock settle a few minutes before straining it again through a sieve lined with a double thickness of wet cheesecloth.

BLACK BEAN SOUP

(Serves 6–8)

This hearty soup is served topped with finely chopped onion in New England and with finely shredded lemon and sliced hard-cooked eggs in Florida.

1 pound (2 cups) dried black beans	¼ cup chopped parsley, or 2 tablespoons parsley flakes
water to cover, to be discarded	2 bay leaves
2 large onions, chopped	1 teaspoon salt
4 ribs celery, chopped	½ teaspoon freshly ground black pepper
¼ cup butter, margarine, or oil	1 ham bone, or shank end
2 quarts cold water	

Soak the beans in water to cover overnight or for at least 5 hours. Discard any "floaters." Drain the beans. In a large kettle, stockpot, or Dutch oven, heat the fat and cook the onions and celery until translucent. Add the drained beans and remaining ingredients. Cover and simmer for 3 hours or more. Remove the ham bone and purée the bean soup in a food mill or blender. Cut up or shred into small pieces any bits of ham meat from the bone and add to the puréed soup. Reheat and serve hot, topped with either more minced onions, sliced hard-cooked eggs, or slivers of lemon.

RUSSIAN-STYLE BORSCHT

(Serves 6)

This hearty soup can be almost considered a meal-in-one dish. It is a flavorful dish of meat, vegetables, and a refreshing cold taste of sour cream—a combination of hot and cold temperatures and smooth and chewable textures all in one dish. It can be cooked over direct heat of embers or on the surface of a hot cookstove.

½ pound bacon	2 No.-2 cans shredded beets and juice
2 to 3 medium-size onions, minced	1 small package sauerkraut, drained
1 clove garlic, minced	3 to 5 medium-size potatoes, peeled and quartered
1 pound beef, cut in 1-inch cubes (round, chuck, or stew meat)	1 teaspoon crumbled thyme
½ cup diced celery	1 teaspoon salt
2 cans concentrated beef broth, or 4 packets beef bouillon	freshly ground black pepper
3 cups water	¼ cup fresh chopped parsley
	1 cup sour cream

In a Dutch oven or heavy saucepan cook the bacon strips until crisp. Drain and set aside (to be crumbled and sprinkled over each portion of borscht when served). Brown the onions, garlic and cut-up beef in the bacon fat. Add the celery, beef broth, water, beets and juice, sauerkraut, potatoes, thyme, salt and pepper. Cover the pan and simmer for 30 minutes or more, or until the celery cooks and the flavors blend. Top each hot serving with bacon bits, parsley, and a dollop of sour cream.

QUICK VEGETABLE SOUP CHILI

(Serves 6)

If you use canned soup and have such general staples as rice, onions, and seasonings, this can be a pantry-shelf type of meal that is easily assembled. All you need in really fresh (or frozen) food is the ground beef. If it's cooked on the surface of the woodstove, you can start preparing it almost as soon as the fire is started.

1 to 2 cups each of homemade vegetable soup and beef stock, *or*

1 10½-ounce can of beef broth and

1 10½-ounce can of vegetable soup

½ to 1 cup chopped, cooked vegetables

½ small onion, minced

1 to 2 carrots, grated or shredded

1 cup canned or fresh tomatoes, crushed

½ cup quick-cooking rice

salt and pepper to taste

Chili Meatballs (*see* following recipe)

Combine all the ingredients in a heavy saucepan, then cook until the rice is tender, about 10 to 15 minutes. Add hot, browned Chili Meatballs to simmer for another 10 to 15 minutes. Serve piping hot.

CHILI MEATBALLS

1 pound ground chuck or round
½ small onion, minced
1 clove garlic, minced
2 to 3 teaspoons chili powder
2 teaspoons salt

¼ cup dried bread crumbs
¼ cup water
2 tablespoons peanut or
　vegetable oil

Mix together all the ingredients except the oils (add more water if the mixture is too stiff) and shape into 1 inch meatballs. Add the oil to a large skillet and brown the meat. Add the browned meatballs to Quick Vegetable Soup Chili and simmer for 10 to 15 minutes.

BAKED BEANS NEW ENGLAND STYLE

(Serves 6–8)

This is a classic method for New England baked beans—either baked in the oven or in the pot over the low heat of a cookstove or suspended in a pot above a wood-burning fire. This dish can "travel" to be partly cooked in the fireplace and/or in the cookstove. Long, slow, even heat is necessary, with an occasional stirring through of the dish and perhaps, from time to time, some water added if the beans seem too dry.

1 pound (2 cups) navy beans,
　soaked overnight in water
¼ pound salt pork, slashed
1 medium-size onion, sliced
more boiling water to cover
1 tablespoon dry mustard

1 tablespoon water
½ teaspoon ground ginger
1 cup dark molasses
1 tablespoon salt
½ teaspoon ground black
　pepper

Drain the soaked beans. Place in a Dutch oven, kettle, or heavy stewpot; cover with boiling water again. Boil the beans until they are tender, for about 1 hour. In a separate bean pot or bowl, combine the dry mustard and tablespoon of water and let stand for 10 minutes to develop the flavor. Stir in the remaining ingredients and combine them with the boiled beans. Cover and cook over low heat directly on the range top or suspended above an open fire, or bake them in a slow oven (300° F.) for 6 to 8 hours. Add water if the beans become too dry.

ORIENTAL EGGPLANT APPETIZER

(Serves 6–8)

The pungent, almost burned flavor and the seasonings make this an appealing appetizer. It is one kind of vegetable that can be cooked in its own skin directly over an open ember fire.

2 medium eggplants, about 2 pounds
1 teaspoon salt
⅛ teaspoon ground black pepper
1 clove garlic, minced fine
1 medium onion, minced fine
4 drops Tabasco

½ teaspoon grated nutmeg
2 tablespoons minced fresh basil, or 1 teaspoon crumbled dry basil
1 tablespoon crumbled parsley flakes
1 lemon, juiced
⅓ cup peanut or vegetable oil

Suspend the unpeeled eggplants in a hinged basket about 4 to 6 inches above the hot embers, or place on a sheet of foil directly on the hot or moderate heated cooking top of the cookstove. Using tongs or a long-handled fork, turn the vegetables from time to time to cook evenly. They should not cook too quickly but should be charred before the cooking time is finished, in about 30 minutes. Remove from the grill or surface when soft and hold the eggplants stem down with a fork to peel and discard the skin. Dice or mash the vegetable in a bowl as finely as possible. Stir in the remaining ingredients and set aside to cool and for the flavors to blend for at least 30 minutes, or cover and cool in the refrigerator before serving. Serve as a dip on toasted bread or crisp crackers.

VEGETABLE MEDLEY

(Serves 6)

This simple vegetable combination is just one dish that is representative of several kinds of combinations that can be prepared as foil-wrapped packages of food. If you will, they can be considered as a kind of disposable casserole after the food contents are eaten.

2 medium onions, thinly sliced	1 tablespoon parsley flakes
4 ribs celery (about 1 cup), slivered	½ teaspoon crumbled thyme
2 medium (about 1 pound) zucchini, sliced	¼ teaspoon crumbled oregano
	1 teaspoon salt
2 yellow summer squash, or 1 10-ounce package frozen corn	freshly ground black pepper
	¼ cup peanut or vegetable oil
3 medium tomatoes, cut	½ large red and/or green pepper, seeded and diced

To make the foil packet for cooking the vegetables, tear off about a 2-foot length of heavy-duty foil (or use a double thickness of the lighter foil), and turn up the sides to form a temporary pan. Slice, cut, and combine all the ingredients, except the red or green diced pepper, which get added only before serving time. The zucchini and squash should be cut in pieces no larger than an inch in size. Use underripe tomatoes. If frozen corn is used, center the block in the packet, as it will have sufficient time to cook along with the other ingredients. To shape the packet, hold the lengthwise edges of the foil together, and fold them over twice (this is known as the "pharmacy fold"). Then double- and triple-fold each of the two ends. Place directly in ash-covered embers, cover with more ashes, and cook for 30 to 45 minutes, depending on the intensity of the fire. It can also be cooked directly on the moderate heat surface of the range, or in the oven.

TOMATO AND EGGPLANT CASSEROLE

(Serves 6)

Another foil-wrapped disposable casserole dish similar to the Vegetable Medley, to be prepared in or on top of the hot embers or in the oven of a cookstove.

1 medium eggplant, about 1½ pounds
boiling water
2 teaspoons salt
2 tablespoons butter or margarine
2 large eggs, beaten
¼ teaspoon ground black pepper

1 tablespoon finely chopped onion
½ teaspoon oregano leaves
8 to 12 crumbled saltines
6 medium-size tomato slices
½ cup grated American cheese

Peel the eggplant and cut into slices ¼-inch thick. Place in a saucepan, covered with a ½ inch of salted boiling water. Cover, bring to the boil again, and cook for 10 minutes or until the eggplant is tender. Drain and mash. Blend in butter or margarine, egg, black pepper, onion, oregano, and saltines. Turn into a large double piece of foil to make 1 packet. Cover the surface with tomato slices. Sprinkle with additional salt, black pepper, and grated cheese. Fold down top and end seals. Bake in ash-covered embers or in a preheated moderate oven (375° F.) for 25 minutes.

STUFFED CUCUMBERS WITH FRESH TOMATO SAUCE

(Serves 6)

6 large, firm cucumbers
1 pound lean beef, ground twice
1 tablespoon butter or margarine
½ cup soft bread crumbs
¾ teaspoon salt
⅛ teaspoon ground black pepper

¾ teaspoon powdered mustard
2 tablespoons finely chopped onion
½ cup grated Parmesan cheese
¼ cup salad oil
1 clove garlic, crushed
Fresh Tomato Sauce (*see following recipe*)

Wash the cucumbers. Cut off the tips and cut each in half. Scoop out the centers with an apple corer, leaving a ¼-inch wall and 1 end of each half closed. Stand open-side down to drain. Brown beef lightly and quickly in melted butter or margarine. Add the next 6 ingredients and mix well. Stuff the cucumbers with this mixture. Combine the oil and garlic and spread in the bottom of double layers of foil that are large enough to make individual foil packets. Add the cucumbers. Bake in the ash-covered embers or in a preheated moderate oven (350° F.) for 45 to 55 minutes. Serve topped with Fresh Tomato Sauce.

FRESH TOMATO SAUCE

2 cups diced fresh tomatoes	¹⁄₁₆ teaspoon ground black
½ cup water	pepper
1½ tablespoons cornstarch	⅛ teaspoon ground oregano
½ teaspoon salt	

Combine all the ingredients and simmer for 10 minutes or until the tomatoes are tender and the sauce has thickened.

HAM AND CHEESE SANDWICHES WITH GREEN TOMATO, EGGPLANT, OR ZUCCHINI

(Serves 6)

You can do this dish on a hot griddle suspended above an open-ember fire in the fireplace. You can also use a griddle or a skillet on top of a hot range.

One of the following vegetables:

3 to 4 green tomatoes, *or*	2 to 4 tablespoons peanut or
1 medium-size, eggplant, about	vegetable oil
1 to 1¼ pounds, *or*	6 slices boiled ham
1 to 1½ pounds zucchini	6 slices Cheddar or Provolone
1 cup flour	cheese
1 teaspoon salt	½ teaspoon finely crumbled
¼ teaspoon celery salt	oregano
freshly ground black pepper	

Cut the green tomatoes, eggplant, or zucchini crosswise into slices about ¼-inch thick. Make at least 12 to 18 slices. Dredge each slice in the flour blended with salt, celery salt, and pepper. Heat the oil on a griddle or in a large, heavy skillet and brown the dredged vegetables on one side, then turn and top each slice with a portion of boiled ham and cheese. Sprinkle the top with oregano. As the second side cooks, the ham and cheese heat through. Serve hot.

BROCCOLI AU GRATIN WITH HAM OR TUNA

(Serves 4 to 6)

This is just one dish which started cooked in a wok and got expanded into a cookstove-oven dish. Note, again, the suggestion of mixing dry mustard *only* with water to release its full flavor.

1 bunch broccoli	½ lemon, juiced
1 teaspoon powdered mustard	1 6½-ounce can tuna fish, *or*
1 tablespoon water	2 cups diced cooked ham
2 tablespoons butter or margarine	½ cup grated cheese (Parmesan, Swiss, or Cheddar)
2 tablespoons flour	½ to ¾ cup crumbled saltine crackers or bread crumbs
2 cups milk	
½ teaspoon salt	1 tablespoon butter or margarine, melted
freshly ground black pepper	

Cook the broccoli in a wok (as described on page 144) and place in a large skillet or baking dish. Prepare the sauce by first mixing the mustard with water, and let it stand for 10 minutes. Set it aside to be stirred into the sauce later. In a small saucepan melt the butter or margarine, blend in the flour, and gradually stir in the milk. Cook for about 7 minutes, or until sauce thickens, stirring constantly with a wooden spoon. Add the mustard, salt and pepper, and lemon juice. Arrange the flaked tuna or diced ham and the grated cheese over the top of the cooked broccoli. Cover with the sauce. Blend the crackers or bread crumbs with the melted butter or margarine and sprinkle over the top of the dish. Bake in a moderate oven (350° F.) for about 30 minutes, or until the cheese melts and the crumbs become nicely brown. Serve hot.

SPICED BAKED WHOLE ONIONS

(Serves 6)

Foil-wrapped packages of food, if properly sealed, are the nearest thing to using a pressure cooker and cook at about five pounds of pressure.

Also, double-layer foil packages can serve as a saucepan on the grill. And to avoid the fish flavors permeating the cast-iron or metal cooking utensil in which a fish is being poached, use a foil pan inside the pot or skillet, with some water inside.

Foil-roasted potatoes, whole onions, corn, and apples are particular favorites of fireplace cooks. Packets of vegetables, and vegetable, meat, or fish combinations also offer countless menu items and varieties.

6 medium-size yellow onions, unpeeled	**1 teaspoon salt**
¼ cup peanut or vegetable oil	**¼ teaspoon ground nutmeg**
1 tablespoon light or dark brown sugar	**¼ teaspoon chili powder**
	pinch of ground cloves
	freshly ground black pepper

Cut the stem end off each onion. Use heavy-duty foil or make double-layer squares of regular foil large enough to encase each onion. Place the unpeeled onion in the center of each square and turn up the sides. Pour on the spiced topping. Make the topping by combining the oil, sugar, salt, and spices. Add this to the onions. Bring up the sides of the foil and twist the tops to make sealed packets. Cook suspended about 4 to 6 inches above hot embers, or directly in ash-covered hot coals, or if cooked on the hearth, a little in front of the burning fire. Turn the packets about every 10 minutes for more even cooking. Onions require about 45 minutes of cooking. To serve, open the packets and, with a fork, spear the whole onion through the cut top, over a dish, and peel off and discard the skin. Return each peeled cooked onion to the juicy spiced sauce in the packets and serve.

SKILLET CREOLE CABBAGE

(Serves 6)

This is either a quick-cooking skillet dish or a foil-wrapped packet type of dish that is easy to assemble—and good for foods that offer year-round availability.

2 tablespoons butter or
  margarine
½ medium onion, chopped
1 small green pepper, seeded
  and chopped
2 ribs celery, thinly sliced
2 cups (3 medium-sized) fresh
  tomatoes

1 quart shredded cabbage
2 teaspoons salt
1 teaspoon sugar
⅛ teaspoon ground black
  pepper

Melt butter or margarine in a 10-inch skillet or in a large double-foil packet. Add the remaining ingredients. Cover or seal top and ends. Cook over moderate heat or over ash-covered embers for about 30 minutes.

GHIVETCH (ROUMANIAN VEGETABLES)

(Serves 8 or 10)

This can be surface or oven-cooked and also prepared as a foil-wrapped packet cooked in the hot embers of an open fire, surrounded by an insulating layer of ashes to keep the food from scorching as it cooks.

2 medium carrots, thinly sliced
1 cup green beans, thinly sliced
  diagonally
2 small potatoes, peeled and
  diced
2 ribs celery, thinly sliced
  diagonally
2 medium tomatoes, quartered
1 small zucchini, thinly sliced
1 small Bermuda onion,
  chopped
½ head cauliflower, broken into
  flowerets
½ red pepper, sliced in thin
  strips

½ green pepper, sliced in thin
  strips
1 10-ounce package frozen
  green peas
⅓ cup peanut or vegetable oil
1 cup beef bouillon
3 cloves garlic, finely minced
2 teaspoons salt
½ bay leaf, crumbled
½ teaspoon crumbled savory or
  thyme
¼ teaspoon crumbled tarragon

Prepare the vegetables. Preheat the oven to 375° F. and mix and put the vegetables into an uncovered oven casserole or baking dish. Heat the oil and add the bouillon, cooking this for 5 minutes with the remaining seasonings. Pour this over the vegetables. Cover the dish and bake until the vegetables are tender, about 1 hour. Stir the vegetables once or twice during cooking.

Note: This dish may also be cooked in a double-thickness foil packet in the ash-coated embers in a fireplace.

SOURMILK OR BUTTERMILK PANCAKE BATTER

(Makes 8 to 12 Cakes)

Here's the pancake recipe that my grandmother used. But more important, note how the griddle is tested for proper baking temperature. And note the variations in making buckwheat cakes.

2 eggs, slightly beaten
1½ cups all-purpose flour
½ teaspoon salt
1 teaspoon sugar
2 teaspoons baking soda

½ teaspoon cream of tartar
1½ cups sour milk or buttermilk
1 tablespoon peanut or
vegetable oil

Test the griddle or skillet for baking temperature by sprinkling a few drops of water on it. If they bounce and disappear, the temperature is correct. But if they evaporate before they bounce, the griddle is too hot and either the griddle should be moved, raised to a higher level, or to a cooler area.

Beat the eggs in a bowl. Combine the dry ingredients and sift them. Blend the milk with the eggs. Stir in the dry ingredients all at once, and when blended beat in the oil. Allow the batter to rest for 30 minutes, or overnight, before baking. Drop or pour batter by large spoonfuls onto a hot griddle or skillet. (If thinner cakes are desired, stir in more liquid.) As soon as bubbles appear at the edges of the cake (in about 1 to 2 minutes), they are ready to be flipped over and baked on the other side.

To make buckwheat cakes the method and ingredients are slightly different. Scald and cool the milk until lukewarm. Add to it 1 package of granulated yeast and stir to dissolve. Stir in the buckwheat flour and salt, only until thoroughly blended. Cover and let stand overnight. Just before baking, substitute 1 tablespoon dark molasses for the sugar, add the remaining ingredients, and bake immediately. (This method is necessary as the buckwheat consistency is heavier.)

Note: To "sour" milk, use ½ teaspoon cider vinegar to every cup of milk; let it stand for about 15 minutes at room temperature.

BASIC BREAD: SKILLET LOAF OR TWISTS

(Makes 1 Loaf or 18 Twists)

This basic bread is made with a simple dough-mixing technique; the recipe turns out a good loaf or roll-like bread twist. It is baked directly over an open fire, or in a reflector oven set up in front of a fire, or on a rack in a preheated Dutch oven, suspended from a danglehook near the hot back wall of the hearth in a long-burning fireplace fire. Note the simple "snap-finger" test against the hot surface of the bread after 45 minutes of baking. If the bread is done and baked through, snapping it will produce a hollow sound.

1 cup milk	1 teaspoon salt
2 tablespoons butter or margarine	1 package granulated yeast
	2 tablespoons lukewarm water
1 tablespoon sugar	3 to 4 cups all-purpose flour

Heat the milk, fat, sugar, and salt until the fat melts. Set the milk mixture aside to cool until lukewarm to the touch. In a large bowl stir and dissolve the yeast and warm water and let stand for about 5 minutes, or until the yeast bubbles. Stir in the milk mixture and 3 cups of the flour until the dough can be pulled away from the sides of the bowl. On a cool work surface, lightly work and knead the dough, adding more flour as is necessary to handle it. Place the dough in bowl and using your hand lightly brush some oil over the top surface. Cover the bowl with a clean towel and set it in a fairly warm place (back shelf on the stove, or in front of the fireplace hearth) away from drafts. Let the dough double in bulk and test by poking it with two fingers: if the indentation stays, the dough is ready to be shaped. Shape and let it double again before baking in a well-greased skillet, or cut into strips to be doubled in bulk and wrapped around green sticks to be baked above a hot-ember fire. The bread loaf may also be baked in a rack in a Dutch oven, turning the utensil several times during baking for uniform doneness. (A loaf should bake in about 45 minutes. To test for doneness, snap fingers against the hot surface—and if a hollow sound is produced, the loaf is done.)

BREAD: WHOLE OR OTHER-GRAIN VARIATIONS

For making whole-wheat bread, or breads that have other more coarse grains (such as cornmeal, oatmeal, etc.) use the same mixing and shaping techniques but double the amounts of milk, fat, sugar, salt, and yeast as given in the preceding recipe. Use the same amount of the whole-grain or other grains. Also, you may wish to combine the regular flour with the whole grains or other grains. If you do this, vary the amounts of milk, sugar, and salt accordingly—but always use twice the amount of yeast called for in the original recipe. You will need to allow almost double the time for the dough to rise.

Some old-timers even skipped using a skillet in which to bake this bread—they merely placed the punched-out dough directly in the not-too-hot ashes, covered or sprinkled a layer of ashes on top and around it, and then piled on hot embers to bake the dough, buried in the fire but partly insulated with ashes, for about 30 minutes. The bread was raked from the fire, brushed free of ashes, and broken into pieces and eaten while hot.

FIREPLACE SKILLET BREAD

2 cups all-purpose flour (or combination of 1 cup whole-wheat flour and 1 cup all-purpose flour)
2 teaspoons double-acting baking powder

1 teaspoon salt
¾ to 1 cup milk, depending on stiffness of dough
1 tablespoon peanut or vegetable oil

Combine all the ingredients and make a stiff dough that can be shaped into a circular mound. Lightly flour it. Using your hand, shape a hole in the center so that it appears like an oversized doughnut. Coat the bottom of a 10- or 12-inch skillet with some oil and place the bread dough in it, directly over hot embers that have been lightly topped with ashes. Turn the bread to brown the bottom as evenly as possible. To bake the top, tilt and brace the skillet at a 45-degree angle to catch the heat from the firebox and fire. Bread will be baked when browned and when it produces a hollow sound when snapped with the fingers. Bread bakes in about 20 to 30 minutes.

CORNSTICKS (RAISED JOHNNY CAKE)

(Makes 10 to 12)

This is a basic cornstick type of recipe. In New England, quite often the baking powder and/or baking soda was eliminated (as often, as well, the egg) to make a thin-sheet type of Johnny Cake that was crisp and crunchy, but quite "spartan" as to ingredients. In the South, more eggs might be added. They were often separated, the whites beaten to soft peaks before folding them into the rich cornmeal egg-yolk mixture. Baked in a soufflélike dish, in an oven, it yields up that delicacy—feather-light Southern Spoon Bread.

RAISED JOHNNY CAKE

1 cup all-purpose flour
1 cup yellow cornmeal
1 tablespoon sugar
2 teaspoons double-acting
  baking powder
1 teaspoon salt

½ teaspoon baking soda
¾ cup buttermilk or sourmilk
  (*see* method on page 126)
1 large egg, lightly beaten
¼ cup melted butter, margarine,
  or salad oil

In a preheated hot oven (425° F.), preheat heavy metal cornstick pans or "gem" muffin pans (fluted tins) and grease them well while preparing the batter. Fill about two-thirds full with the batter made as follows:

In a large bowl blend the dry ingredients together. Add the egg, milk, and melted butter or margarine (or oil) and mix only enough to blend. Pour the batter into the cornstick or muffin pans and bake in a hot oven for about 20 minutes.

Note: The batter may also be baked for about 30 minutes as a skillet cake in a 12-inch or larger preheated well-greased skillet.

NEW ENGLAND SKILLET CAKE

(Makes 1 10- or 12-inch Cake)

This is similar to the Johnny Cake.

1 cup yellow cornmeal	½ teaspoon salt
1 tablespoon fat	1 cup boiling water

Heat a large cast-iron skillet and grease the inside bottom (or if skillet has an outside rimmed bottom, grease that and bake the Johnny Cake into a very thin layer on the bottom outside of the preheated pan). Mix all the ingredients and pour the batter onto the hot pan, smoothing or patting it out into a very thin layer. Bake it over a high heat or in a hot oven (400° F.) for about 10 to 15 minutes. If baked over a fireplace or stove embers, suspend or balance the pan about 4 inches above the coals.

STEAMED BROWN BREAD

(Makes 2 Loaves)

Done in a kettle or Dutch oven, in large fruit-juice cans, or in two tubular pans.

1 cup sifted all-purpose flour	2 cups yellow cornmeal
1 teaspoon baking soda	1 cup seedless raisins
1 teaspoon ground cinnamon	2 cups buttermilk or sourmilk
1 teaspoon ground allspice	(*see* method on page 126)
1 teaspoon salt	1 cup dark molasses
1 cup uncooked oatmeal	

Into a large bowl sift together the flour, soda, spices, and salt. Lightly stir in the oatmeal and cornmeal. For later use, reserve about 2 tablespoons of the dry ingredients to mix with the raisins. Stir in the milk and molasses to the dry ingredients and then blend in the coated raisins.

Grease and lightly flour the empty, clean fruit-juice cans and pour in the batter. Form covers for the cans with heavy-duty foil, or a double layer of foil, and tie the tops on with strong string. Place on a rack in a large deep kettle and pour in enough boiling water to immerse the cans halfway. Cover and steam for 3 hours. Remove from water, uncover, and cool for about 30 minutes before removing from cans.

SUET PUDDING

(Makes 1 ½ quarts Pudding)

This is a colonial recipe and its ingredients are hearty and healthy—a no-nonsense dessert that added needed calories and energy for the physically active life of those days. Usually it was served topped with a delicate boiled custard egg sauce, laced with brandy, rum, or (a rarity in colonial days, but possible) lemon.

3 cups sifted all-purpose flour
⅓ to ½ pound suet, ground or
    finely minced
1 cup ground or minced
    seedless raisins

1 cup dark molasses
1 ½ teaspoons baking soda
1 cup milk

In a large bowl toss together the flour, suet, and raisins. Combine the molasses and soda to a foamy consistency. Add this to the flour mixture, along with the milk, and stir to blend. Pour immediately into a well-greased mold and cover. Put the mold, top-side up, in a Dutch oven or kettle with a rack about 2 or more inches off the bottom. Add enough boiling water to just below the mold, cover the utensil, and steam for 4 hours or more. Check the water level occasionally.

INDIAN PUDDING

(Serves 6)

Another rib-sticker from colonial days, but served with rum raisin or any regular ice cream today, it's a delicious and special dessert.

2 cups hot milk
¼ cup yellow cornmeal
½ teaspoon salt
½ teaspoon ground nutmeg
½ teaspoon ground ginger
½ teaspoon ground cinnamon

¼ teaspoon baking soda
½ cup dark molasses
1 cup milk
heavy cream, whipped, *or* ice
    cream (optional)

In a Dutch oven or heavy skillet heat the milk and gradually stir in the cornmeal. Continue to stir and cook over low heat until thick, about 15 minutes. Remove from the heat and blend in the next five ingredients. Stir in the molasses and milk. Cover and return to the heat to cook—very slowly. (If in a fireplace, suspend high above the heat. If on a wood stove, place a trivet under the pan or position on the surface area that is warm, or in a slow oven (250°–275° F.) for about 2 hours more. Serve warm with whipped cream or ice cream, if desired.

SPICED CHOCOLATE CAKE

(Makes 1 9- to 10-inch Cake)

This cake is mixed in the same dish in which it is baked and is a great show-off dessert done in a Dutch oven suspended directly over an open fire or on top of the range.

1½ cups all-purpose flour	1 cup light-brown sugar
¼ cup cocoa	¼ cup vegetable oil
1 teaspoon baking soda	1 square (2-ounces)
1 teaspoon ground cinnamon	unsweetened chocolate,
½ teaspoon ground allspice	melted
½ teaspoon salt	1 tablespoon cider vinegar
¼ teaspoon ground cloves	1 cup milk

In a mixing bowl, sift together the flour, cocoa, and dry ingredients, and then blend in the sugar. Make a well in the center of the flour mixture and add, all at once, the oil, melted chocolate, vinegar, and milk. Stir to blend thoroughly. Pour the batter into a 9- or 10-inch cake pan and bake in a regular oven, or pour into a cast-iron Dutch oven that has been preheated to moderate oven temperature (350° F) and bake for 45 minutes or more, or until a broom straw or toothpick comes out clean when inserted in the center. Cut and serve from the pan or turn out, cool, and frost with the cream cheese mixture on page 134.

Note: You can mix the batter in the baking pan in which the cake is to bake.

SPICY APPLE UPSIDE-DOWN SKILLET CAKE

(Makes 1 10- to 12-Inch Cake)

While this recipe is for an apple upside-down cake, you can use other fruit in season, such as fresh peaches, blueberries, or drained, canned pineapple rounds or chunks. *A hint:* To make it easier to turn the finished upside-down cake out of the skillet or pan, line the interior and sides of the pan with a single or double layer of foil, pushing it to the shape of the pan.

2 or 3 tart baking apples
⅓ cup melted butter or
    margarine
1 cup dark-brown sugar
2½ cups sifted all-purpose flour
1 tablespoon sugar
1¼ teaspoons baking soda
1 teaspoon salt
1½ teaspoons ground ginger
½ teaspoon ground allspice

½ teaspoon ground cinnamon
1 large egg
1 cup dark molasses
1¼ cups hot milk
⅓ cup vegetable oil
1 cup heavy cream, whipped
    (optional)
1 teaspoon sugar (optional)
grated nutmeg (optional)

While butter or margarine melts in the bottom of a heavy 10- or 12-inch skillet, peel, core, and cut the apples crosswise into rings or make slices about ½-inch thick. Sprinkle brown sugar into skillet and arrange the sliced apples on top. In a bowl stir the dry ingredients to blend before beating in the egg, molasses, and hot milk. Stir in the vegetable oil. Pour or spoon the batter over the apples and bake suspended above hot embers of a fire or in a preheated slow oven (325° F.), for about 45 minutes, or until a toothpick or straw comes out clean when inserted in the center. Cool in skillet for about 5 minutes. To serve, invert a platter or plate over the skillet to remove the cake. If desired, serve with a dollop of whipped cream sweetened with sugar. Also, sprinkle on some grated nutmeg.

PEACH, APPLE, OR BANANA FRAZE

(Serves 6)

This dessert is adapted from colonial days. It is sliced fruit in a wine-laced egg batter, fried in a spider or skillet (or on an iron or soapstone griddle) in a small amount of butter or margarine. Served hot and sprinkled with confectioners' sugar, it's a delicious dish.

3 to 6 firm fresh peaches, *or*
3 large, firm tart apples, *or*
3 underripe bananas
2 eggs, lightly beaten
½ teaspoon salt
½ teaspoon sugar
1 cup milk

¼ to ½ cup wine—medium-dry
    Sherry or Sauterne
½ to ¾ cup flour
1 tablespoon vegetable oil
2 to 4 tablespoons butter or
    margarine

133

Peel all the fruit, remove the stones from peaches if used, or the cores from the apples. Cut the fruit into slices a little less than ½-inch thick. Dredge the pieces in the wine-laced batter. To prepare the batter, beat together the egg, salt, sugar, milk, and wine and blend in the flour and tablespoon of oil to make a smooth batter.

Note: The amount of flour will depend on the thickness desired and what consistency will cling to the fruit; for example, the juicier sliced fruits require a thicker batter.

Heat a griddle or skillet and coat lightly with butter or margarine; quickly brown the batter-dipped fruit pieces and serve, piping hot, sprinkled with confectioners' sugar.

CREAM CHEESE FROSTING

(Makes about 1½ Cups Frosting)

Good on French toast, also as a topping for cakes, and for apple and fruit desserts.

3 ounce-package cream cheese
1 tablespoon milk or cream
1/16 teaspoon salt

1 teaspoon vanilla extract
2 cups confectioners' sugar

Blend together the cream cheese and milk. Combine to spreading consistency with remaining ingredients. If a thinner frosting is desired, add a little more milk.

CHEDDAR CHEESE FONDUE

(Serves 6)

This is a dish that requires really low, slow heat and a long time to heat without separating. It is a particularly good dish to do on top of one of those two-step level woodstoves whose top surfaces are especially used for simple, small cooking tasks.

1½ teaspoons dry mustard
1 tablespoon water
1 teaspoon Worcestershire
    sauce (optional)
¼ cup butter or margarine
⅓ cup all-purpose flour
½ teaspoon salt

½ teaspoon freshly ground
    black pepper
2 cups milk
3 cups grated sharp Cheddar
12 slices toasted bread, or
    cubed, for dunking

First prepare the mustard by mixing together the dry mustard with the water to a smooth paste. Add the Worcestershire, if desired. Allow the mustard to stand for at least 10 minutes before using.

In large, heavy saucepan (or pan that sits within another, as an improvised double boiler) melt the butter or margarine and blend in the flour, salt, and pepper. Gradually stir in the milk. Move the pan to an area where there is low heat and stir and cook the milk sauce for about 10 to 15 minutes, or until it is of medium thickness. If possible, place over a pan of just simmering water (or move to a warm cooking area) and stir in the cheese to cook until it is all melted. Add the prepared mustard. Serve immediately over toasted bread slices or set out toasted bread cubes and forks for each person to dunk into the fondue.

CAFÉ BRÛLOT

(Serves 6 to 8)

This is a different technique than is ordinarily used in making Café Brulot; it is adapted for fireplace cooking and for safety's sake. In this recipe the hot coffee is made elsewhere and poured *into* the ignited brandy-spice mix.

6 to 8 cups strong, hot black coffee	peel from 1 orange
1 2-inch stick cinnamon	peel from ½ lemon
1 vanilla bean, or 1 teaspoon extract	1 tablespoon sugar
	1 cup brandy
4 whole cloves	¼ cup Cointreau (optional)
	1 lump sugar

Keep the coffee hot. In a separate pan that is easy to pour from, combine the remaining ingredients, except the lump of sugar. (Reserve the lump to be wet down with some of the brandy in a spoon, gently heated and ignited, used later as a lighter for the flavored brandy.) Heat and stir the spice, fruit peel, and brandy mixture until the sugar dissolves. Holding the pan away from you (let the flames go up the chimney if you are doing this in the fireplace), ignite it with the lighted sugar lump and stir in the hot coffee. Continue to stir until the flames go out. Pour immediately into demitasse or regular cups and serve.

Cooking with a Wok

Chinese food is not the only thing you can cook in a wok. It is a very useful pan to have for both fireplace and woodstove, to cook directly over a fire for stir-frying and for steaming or baking foods. It can be used like a shallow Dutch oven, with a rack inside, a tight-fitting cover, and it is then a great piece of equipment for small baking tasks. When used as a skillet it is especially adaptable to cook such items as bacon. Bacon can be arranged along the sloping sides, and as it cooks the fat drains from it into the bottom of the wok, leaving the bacon crisp and well done.

The wok makes possible many wonderful one-dish meals. It is an easier piece of equipment to handle than the Dutch oven or stockpots. As the steaming or stir-frying procedure is accomplished, the various ingredients that make up the final dish can either be cooked and added according to the timing for "doneness" or the foods can be cooked individually, the pan emptied, and the contents set aside for a later mixing before serving.

Wok cooking allows for the flavors of different ingredients to blend together and thus add to the overall taste of the dish. Also, wok cooking does not overcook foods—and more nutritive values are retained. The fact that we are starting to ingest smaller quantities of meats, due in part to the high costs of meats as well as the knowledge that we do not need as much in our diets, has made us realize the value of wok cooking.

Some woks are still made of cast iron. But most of them are of other metals. Stainless steel is heavier and more durable than sheet steel.

Whatever kind you purchase, be certain that the handles are metal and therefore won't burn. Woks are conical in shape, and for this reason alone they are both economical of fuel and fat if you are doing any deep-frying. Woks, regardless of their metal, also have to be "seasoned" in the same way that cast iron is seasoned.

When purchasing the wok, buy a bamboo scrubber—it looks something like a short reversible whisk broom—which is nonabrasive and with soap and water cleans the pan very well. Also, if you plan much cooking in a wok, treat yourself to a brass or stainless-steel strainer and ladle with handles, which do not transmit heat, to turn the foods more easily.

Always buy a wok that has a ring on which it can stand and be supported over the hot embers. It is also beneficial to select a wok that has a metal tray inset for steaming foods. As in all pans selected, be certain that the top has a tight-fitting cover. One great advantage in wok cooking is that the pan can cook a large quantity of food, yet it is ideal for cooking one or two portions. For example, it is much easier to turn out a twelve-egg omelet by tilting the hot wok from side to side with the beaten egg-mixture inside than to handle a very large skillet to cook such a large quantity for an omelet. Another example of its flexibility is when steaming or baking a large fish. The fish can be placed on the rack and slightly curled around; otherwise you need an expensive and large piece of equipment rarely used, such as a fish poacher.

STIR-FRY IN A WOK

The basic routine for stir-frying in a wok is to know the order in which foods cook (timing) and when to add or cook them in the large pan in the small amount of vegetable oil that keeps the pieces from sticking to the sloping sides of the pan.

The suggested routine is as follows:
1. First cook in the hot oil any food to be browned, such as nuts, chopped onions, or certain meats; and any flavorings such as whole garlic cloves or slivers of gingerroot, and seasonings that require heat to also release the aroma, such as curry powder or a blend of what is known as the Oriental five spices. (*Note:* Ground gingerroot and/or minced or finely chopped garlic may be left in the dish as an added ingredient.)
2. Pork, chicken, and beef bite-size pieces may be stir-fried next, and either removed from the pan before proceeding to cook the rest of the ingredients, or the pieces may be pushed up along

the sloping sides while the remainder of the ingredients are cooked.

3. Stir-fry each vegetable separately, starting with the ones that require longest cooking time. As they cook, either push them up the sloping sides; or if the quantity becomes too large for the wok, remove the meats and vegetables to be mixed together in the pan and reheated just before serving.
4. Stir-fry fast-cooking meats such as thinly shredded chicken and seafood last, as they require less cooking time.
5. Mix the vegetables and meats.
6. Blend in and cook the gravy, wine, and/or cornstarch sauces.
7. Add browned whole, slivered, or chopped nuts or crunchy items just before serving; otherwise they become soggy.

Note: If gingerroot or whole garlic clove(s) have been heated in the oil and discarded, *do not* use these again in either the marinade or grated or minced as an ingredient.

Examples of Cooking Time for Some Stir-Fried Ingredients

Nuts to brown	1 to 2 minutes
Most meats	3 to 4 minutes
Most seafoods	2 to 3 minutes
Shredded green beans	2 to 3 minutes
Snow pea pods	1 to 2 minutes
Shredded carrots	1 to 2 minutes
Sliced celery	1 to 2 minutes
Green pepper cubes	1 minute or less
Bean sprouts	1 to 2 minutes
Chinese (celery) cabbage	2 to 3 minutes
Cornstarch gravy	until it clears, about 2 minutes

Unless you have more than one wok, we suggest you plan on one stir-fried dish at a meal, along with rice or noodles and a salad and dessert. You may add other main-course foods such as a meat dish and serve an all-vegetable wok dish if you wish; otherwise use two woks—one for a more highly seasoned dish and one for a milder one, such as a pork or chicken dish, plus a seafood dish. One pound of meat or seafood is a satisfactory amount to serve 6 people; allow more for more hearty appetites.

WOK-COOKING GUIDE

In combining quantities, the following is a guide:

1. To every 2 to 4 cups of vegetables, use 1 pound of meat, chicken, or seafood.
2. The sauces, such as soy sauce, Sherry, or black bean sauce vary in amounts of 2 to 4 tablespoonfuls, depending on flavor desired. A good combination is all three.
3. Use 1 tablespoon of cornstarch to thicken ½ cup of liquid—use more of each if more gravy is desired.
4. Use fresh vegetables as much as possible for crispness and food value.
5. A basic marinade for a pound of meat, chicken, or fish may con-

sist of a blend of 3 tablespoons soy sauce with 3 tablespoons Sherry or white wine and 1 tablespoon of cornstarch or vinegar.

6. Bite-size pieces of foods in stir-fry make it easier to eat and decreases the cooking time by increasing the amount of surface area exposed to the heat. The faster food cooks, the more nutrients it retains; the seasonings and sauces gain in flavor; and the meats are more tender.

7. *Cutting* foods for stir-frying:

Straight cuts

Some meats such as beef, pork, ham, and most cooked meats.
Fleshy vegetables—i.e., bamboo shoots, mushrooms, water chestnuts.

Diagonal

Firm, stalk vegetables—celery, carrots, asparagus, chives, cabbage.
Flank steak, against grain.
Chicken.

Roll

Cylindrical vegetables—carrots, asparagus.

Shredding

Cut lengthwise, sliced, stacked, and cut lengthwise again, making matchstick-size meats and stalk vegetables; also green beans.

Cubing

Bite-size pieces of meats, onions, and green peppers.

Mincing (chopping fine)

As small pieces as possible.

BASIC INGREDIENTS FOR WOK COOKING

We recognize that in most markets Oriental foods are not plentiful. But wok dishes can be made with American foods cooked in the Oriental manner. Recipes for stir-fried wok dishes are innumerable. Both the traditional Chinese dishes and the interested American cooks of today can create a different one-dish meal with ingenuity. Follow the general guide and stir-fry techniques and almost every dish will be an appetizing variation on the basic theme.

Broth: As chicken used in wok cooking is always "boned and skinned," chicken broth is easily prepared from these bones and skins that are always removed, placed in a pan, and covered with water and simmered for about 2 hours. The broth is strained into a glass container, cooled, covered, refrigerated, and will keep for about a week. (Note: Broth often gels but will re-liquify at room temperature or when heated.)

Oil: Use only vegetable oil and peanut oil especially, as these oils do not burn or smoke at the necessary very high cooking temperatures for stir-frying.

Cornstarch: This always has to be mixed into a thin paste with a little water before stirring it into hot ingredients. As a thickening agent for sauces and gravies, it must be stirred to prevent lumps as it heats.

Chinese Vegetables Easily Purchased

Bamboo Shoots: Even canned retain crispness.

Bean Sprouts: Also wheat and other sprouts are good, but many people grow their own.

Mung Beans: They are obtainable canned and, in city markets, fresh. Growing your own in 3 or 4 days is less expensive and easy to do: Buy dried green mung beans at "health" or "natural food" stores. Cover ⅓ to ½ cup beans with about 1 quart water in a wide-mouth quart jar and soak overnight. Drain off the water and cover the top of the jar with a wet piece of cheesecloth before placing in a dark cabinet at room temperature for 3 to 4 days. During the storing time, rinse the beans and drain off the excess water at least twice a day, draining through the cloth cover. When beans are 1 to 2 inches long, cover the jar with a lid and refrigerate (to stop their growth) until needed. They can be stored for nearly a week.

Water Chestnuts: Canned and once opened may be stored in a jar for up to a month, covered with water (which should be changed every day or so). Jerusalem artichokes may be substituted for the water chestnuts.

Garlic: If grated or minced may be left as an ingredient in the dish, but if whole, it must be removed after flavoring the hot oil.

Fresh Gingerroot vs. Ground Ginger: 1 teaspoon of grated fresh gingerroot is about equal in flavor to ¼ teaspoon ground ginger. If grated or ground is used, it may be left in the dish; but if sliced gingerroot is used, remove it from the hot oil.

Chinese Cabbage: (bok choy) Now fairly available in most supermarkets. If covered and refrigerated, it keeps about one week. It has dark-green leaves.

Snow Pea Pods: Expensive if purchased frozen.

Non-Oriental Vegetables and Fruits for Wok Cooking:

Cucumbers: May be substituted for green and crisp, zucchini or peapods to give interesting texture.

Green and Red Bell Peppers

Carrots

Green Beans

Regular Peas

Asparagus

Celery

Tomatoes—Cherry and regular.

Mushrooms

Scallions—Tops and roots.

Onions

Nuts—Almonds (dishes such as chicken, pork and seafood)
   Cashews (chicken or beef)
   Walnuts (beef) unsalted, whole, slivered and/or chopped.

Meats

Beef: Use less tender cuts as they are usually sliced across the grain or cubed and cooked quickly over high heat, helping to tenderize, especially when marinated.

Port: Shoulder and leg cuts, if lean, are good buys. All cuts may be used.

Chicken: Boned breast meat, slivered, or cut into bite-size pieces are best and most tender for stir-fried chicken dishes.

Seafood: Shrimp, clams, oysters, lobsters, and lobster tails available fresh or frozen and canned are all satisfactory if not overcooked.

Fish: May be cut up and gently poached, but steaming of steaks or whole fish is much preferred. Never stir-fry, as they become too tough and also break apart.

Soy Sauce: For best flavor only buy *imported*, dark, for use as an ingredient.

Dry Wine: Use good table variety dry Sherry for beef and pork. And use a good table variety dry white wine for chicken and fish.

Wok cooking offers not only Oriental-type dishes but can include many Indian dishes, particularly the ones that use curry powder and other exotic blends of ground spices—as the technique of releasing the flavors and aromas in the hot oil is similar to the way foods are cooked in India. Beef Stroganoff is a typical dish suited for wok cookery. Along with a typical Chinese dish we also include recipes for a simple, plain omelet, and some suggested variations on it, and a recipe for a Tandoori Chicken (Indian) and a Beef Stroganoff.

Try these in your wok heated over hot embers in either your fireplace or, with its rounded bottom resting over the hottest area of one of the unlidded concentric holes in your cookstove.

For your own convenience and ease in procedure, be sure to set up the trays of ingredients and any tools needed and have them handy, as wok cooking is fast.

12-EGG OMELET

(Serves 6)

12 eggs
¼ cup water
1 teaspoon salt

freshly ground black pepper
3 tablespoons peanut or
vegetable oil

For a plain egg omelet, beat together eggs, water, salt and pepper. Place the wok over the heat and add the peanut or vegetable oil. When it heats, swirl the wok to coat the sloping sides with the oil. Add the beaten eggs and tilt the wok for the liquid to be in contact with all the sides. Work rapidly and stir down the cooked egg mixture until it begins to set. When the omelet is set, loosen the edges, fold over in half, and slide it onto a warm platter.

Omelet Variations

1. If chopped scallions and/or sliced fresh mushrooms are used, they should be slightly stir-fried in the hot oil, removed, and reserved to be added to the set or nearly set omelet mixture just before sliding it out of the wok. For a 12-egg omelet use ½ cup of chopped scallions and/or ½ cup of sliced mushrooms.
2. Foods that can be added to the omelet just before folding and sliding onto a platter from the wok are:

> Finely chopped watercress or parsley
> Shredded or finely grated Gruyère, Swiss, or Parmesan cheese
> Finely diced cooked ham
> Crumbled cooked bits of bacon
> Finely chopped green pepper
> Diced, peeled fresh tomatoes
> Bean sprouts

Suggestions

The amounts of one, or a combination, of the above varied ingredients should not exceed a total of more than 1 or 1½ cups added to the basic quantity of the prepared 12-egg omelet. For example, about a ½ cup of either diced cooked ham or crumbled bacon and a ½ cup of the finely chopped green pepper, plus (if desired) no more than a ½ cup of either shredded or grated cheese or diced tomatoes.

142

WOK BEEF STROGANOFF

(Serves 6)

1 pound potatoes, peeled and
   julienned (matchstick size)
1 teaspoon salt
2 quarts cold water
1 tray icecubes
¼ cup vegetable oil
1 large onion, sliced
½ pound mushrooms, sliced
1½ pounds lean beef, cut into
   strips ¼-inch thick by
   3 inches long

¼ cup flour
1 teaspoon salt
¼ teaspoon freshly ground
   black pepper
1 cup sour cream
1 8-ounce can tomato puree

Peel and cut up the potatoes into matchstick size and immediately plunge them into a bowl of the salted cold water and ice cubes. Let them soak and crisp for about 30 minutes. If the water becomes very cloudy, drain, and repeat the procedure with fresh ice cubes and cold water over the cut potatoes. (This may be necessary if the potatoes have a high starch content.) Just before heating the oil in the wok, thoroughly drain off the water from the potatoes, place them on a clean cloth towel, and remove any excess water by patting and rolling the towel-wrapped potatoes.

Just as the oil starts to smoke in the wok, swirl the pan slightly to coat the sloping sides. With a long-handled, slotted ladle, spoon about one-third or half the quantity of the potatoes into the wok. The water clinging to them and in them will cause a lot of bubbling and steam. Be careful not to get burned. With the ladle quickly turn and stir the potatoes, which will brown in about 5 minutes. Lift them out to a rack or paper toweling to drain. Repeat the procedure and cook the remainder. Reserve them to serve with the Stroganoff.

In the remaining oil (you may have to add another tablespoon or so), cook the sliced onion until transparent. Remove, and then stir-fry the sliced mushrooms for about 3 minutes; set aside. Add a few slivers of beef which have been dredged in the seasoned flour; brown them in the oil. Return the cooked onions and mushrooms to the wok. In a separate bowl, blend together the sour cream and tomato puree and stir this into the hot ingredients. Continue to stir and heat through. Serve immediately with the potato sticks.

TANDOORI CHICKEN

(Serves 6)

3 chicken breasts, skinned,
  boned, and halved
2 cups yogurt
1 teaspoon salt
¼ cup peanut or vegetable oil
2 cups sliced onions
1 clove garlic, minced

½ teaspoon cayenne
½ teaspoon ground cardamom
1 teaspoon ground cumin
1 tablespoon ground coriander
4 to 5 black peppercorns
1 lemon or lime, juiced
4 to 6 cups cooked rice, hot

Soak skinned and boned chicken halves for about 2 hours in the yogurt-salt combination. Occasionally turn the chicken pieces as they marinate. Heat the oil in the wok and quickly brown the drained chicken pieces. (Reserve the yogurt to be added at the end of the cooking time to be just heated through as a sauce.) After the chicken browns, set it aside and cook the onions and garlic in the hot oil until translucent and return the chicken pieces to the pan. Blend the spices in a small container and sprinkle them over the chicken and onions. Cover and cook for about 30 minutes or until the chicken is fork-tender. Add the lemon or lime juice and spoon the yogurt over the cooked chicken combination. Cover and heat through. Serve with the hot rice.

STIR-FRY BROCCOLI-MUSHROOMS

(Serves 6)

1 garlic clove, whole
2 slices fresh gingerroot, or ¼
  teaspoon ground ginger
3 tablespoons peanut or
  vegetable oil
1 bunch fresh broccoli or 1
  package frozen, defrosted

¼ pound mushrooms, sliced
1 tablespoon cornstarch
1 tablespoon soy sauce
½ cup water
½ teaspoon salt

Heat the oil in the wok and flavor it by browning the garlic clove and gingerroot. Meanwhile, prepare the broccoli by breaking off the flowerets and cutting the branch stems into thin matchstick-size pieces. Break the flowerets apart into bite-size clusters. Slice the mushrooms into approximately the same size pieces as the broccoli. Remove the garlic and gingerroot from the hot oil in the wok and discard. Add the broccoli stems to the wok and stir-fry for a minute or more, then add the flowerets and continue to stir-fry. Push the broccoli up along the sloping sides and add the mushrooms. Combine the cornstarch and soy sauce in the water and pour over the broccoli-mushroom mixture. Sprinkle on the salt and cover the wok and steam the vegetables for about 3 minutes. Do not overcook the broccoli. It should be crisp and bright green, but heated through.

STEAMED FISH CHINESE STYLE

(Serves 6)

**3 to 6 whole fish, cleaned but
   heads and tails left on (see
   Note)**
2 teaspoons salt
**¼ pound mushrooms, sliced or
   chopped**
3 tablespoons soy sauce
**3 tablespoons dry Sherry or dry
   white wine**

2 teaspoons sugar
**3 or 4 scallions, cut into 2-inch
   lengths, including tops**
**2 tablespoons shredded, peeled
   gingerroot**
12 whole shrimp, unpeeled

Wash the fish in cold water and pat dry. Through outside fleshy part of both sides of fish, make shallow diagonal cuts about every inch. Sprinkle the fish, inside and out with the salt. Lay the fish on a heat-proof dish that is slightly smaller in diameter than the sloping sides of the wok, so that it rests on a ring or steamer rack of the wok. Add the chopped mushrooms on top of the fish, and pour in the blended combination of soy sauce, wine, and sugar. Arrange the pieces of scallions and gingerroot on top of the fish. Surround the fish with whole shrimp. Pour in boiling water to within an inch of the platter. When the water boils again, cover the wok and steam the fish for 15 to 20 minutes or until the fish just flakes easily when a fork is inserted. Serve from the steaming platter.

As an aid in removing the platter, a layer of cheesecloth or clean muslin under the platter may help in lifting it from the wok.

Note: Use whole flounder, trout, bass, or perch—and fish fillets or fish steaks may also be cooked this way, but require less cooking time.

HOT VEGETABLE SALAD (CHINESE)

(Serves 6)

2 tablespoons olive or salad oil
2 to 3 ribs celery, cut crosswise
   into thin diagonals
2 cucumbers, peeled and cut
   into bite-size chunks
4 to 5 scallions, and most of
   their tops, cut crosswise into
   rounds
1 small can bean sprouts, rinsed
   and drained

2 underripe tomatoes, peeled
   and cut into eighths
1 green pepper, seeds removed,
   cut into thin strips
1 cup beef stock, or bouillon
½ teaspoon salt
1 tablespoon cornstarch
1 tablespoon soy sauce
3 tablespoons water
1 head iceberg lettuce,
   shredded

Heat the wok until *very* hot. (*Note:* The entire cooking of all the vegetables should be over high heat, and stir-fried while cooking for 2 to 5 minutes for each vegetable.) The technique is to push each vegetable to one side (or the sides of the pan) before adding a new one to be cooked quickly in the center (hottest) of the pan. After cooking all the vegetables, push to one side and pour in a mixture of the beef bouillon, salt, cornstarch, soy sauce, and water. Stir until the sauce clears and mix with the vegetables. Serve over the shredded lettuce.

REFERENCES

Sources

All Nighter Stove Works, Inc., 80 Commerce Street, Glastonbury, CT 06033.

Alpine Industries, Inc., One Perimeter Road, P.O. Box 3055, Manchester, NH 03105.

Ashley Automatic Heater Co., Box 730, Sheffield, AL 35660.

Atlanta Stove Works, Box 5254, Atlanta, GA 30307 (full line).

Autocrat Corps, New Athens, IL 62264.

Bowdud Arrow Imports, 14 Arrow Street, Cambridge, MA 02138.

Boy Scouts of America, National Supply Service (cookware), 308 Fifth Ave., New York, NY 10001.

Brown Stove Works, Inc., Box 490, Cleveland, TN 37311.

C & D Distributors, Inc., Box 715, Old Saybrook, CT 06475.

The Cawley Stove Co., Inc., 27 North Washington Street, Boyertown, PA 19512.

Cumberland General Store, Route 3, Grossville, TN 38555 (stoves and cookware).

Elmira Stove Works, 22 Church Street West, Elmira, Ontario, Canada N3B 1M4.

Fatsco, Fair Avenue, Benton Harbor, MI 49022 (small stoves: cooking-heating).

Fisher Stoves, Inc., River Road, Route 3, Bow, NH 03301.

Foresight Enterprises, Inc., 343 Lumisor Street, Ludlow, MA 01056 (N-E-R-G Saver with Cook Top).

Frontier Wood Stoves, J & J Enterprises, 4065 West 11th Avenue, Eugene, OR 97402.

Greenbriar Products, Box 473, Spring Green, WI 53588.

Griswold, Countryside Catalog, 312 Portland Road, Waterloo, WI 53594 (cookware).

Hayes-Te-Equipment Corp., P.O. Box 266-2 D, Unionville, CT 06085.

J. C. Penney, Headquarters, 1301 Avenue of the Americas, New York, N.Y. 10019.

Kickapoo Stove Works, Main Street, La Fargo, WI 54639.

King Stove & Range Co., Box 730 Sheffield, AL 35660.

Kristia Associates, Box 1561, Portland, ME 04104 (full line: imports from Norway).

Lange Range, American Distributor, Box 72, Olstead, NH 03602 (imports: Scandinavia and TIBA).

L. L. Bean, Freeport, ME 04032 (stoves and cookware).

Locke Stove Co., 114 West 11th Street, Kansas City, MO 64105.

Louisville Tin & Stove Co., Box 1079, Louisville, KY 40201.

Lyons Supply Co., Inc., One Perimeter Road, P.O. Box 5035, Manchester, NH 03105.

Maleable Iron Range Co., Beaver Dam, WI 53916.

MALM Fireplaces, Inc., 368 Yolanda Avenue, Santa Rosa, CA 95404.

Marathon Heater Co., Inc., Box 167, Marathon, NY 13803.

Martin Industries, Sheffield, AL 35660.

Montgomery Ward, *see* catalog.

Mother Earth News, Box 70, Hendersonville, NC 28739.

Mother's General Store, Box 506, Flat Rock, NC 28739 (stoves and cookware).

Pioneer Lamp and Stove Co., 75 Yesler, Seattle, WA 98104.

Portland Franklin Stove Foundry Inc., Box 1156, Portland, ME 04104 (full line).

Preston Distributing Co., 1 Whidden Street, Lowell, MA 01852 (Portland stoves, cookware).

Radiant Grate, Inc., 31 Morgan Park, Linton, CT 06413 (grates and cooking accessories).

Riteway Manufacturing Co. (Division of Sarco Corp.), Box 6, Harrisonburg, VA 22801.

Scott Foundry, 3159 West 68th Street, Cleveland, OH 44102 (heavy aluminum ware).

Sears & Roebuck, *see* catalog.

Self-Sufficiency Products, 1 Appleton Square, Minneapolis, MN 55420.

Shipmate Stove Division (Richmond Ring Co.), Sanderton, PA 18964.

Vermont Casting, Inc., Dept. WD–2, Randolph, VT 05060.

Vermont Soapstone Co., Inc., Perkinsville, VT 05151 (stoves and griddles).

Vermont Woodstove Co., 307 Elm Street, Bennington, VT 05201.

Wagner Ironware, General Housewares (Cookware), P.O. 4066, 1566 Beech Street, Terre Haute, IN 47804.

Washington Stove Works, Box 687, Everett, WA 98206.

Weir Stove Co., Taunton, MA 02780 (old-time manufacturing iron stoves and parts).

W. F. Landers Co., Box 211, Springfield, MA 01101 (wide assortment of domestic and imports; all kinds of accessories), "Lanco" appliances and equipment.

Wilton Stove Works, 33 Danbury Road, Wilton, CT 06807 (steel and cookrange).

Winnwood Industries, 4200 Birmingham Road, Kansas City, KS 64117 (complete fireplace equipment).

Bibliography

Anderson, Jean. *Recipes from American Restored Villages.* New York: Doubleday, 1973.

Bates, Joseph D. *Outdoor Cooks' Bible.* New York: Doubleday, 1964.

Brush, Warren D., and Collingwood, Gil. *Knowing Your Trees.* Revised edition. The American Forestry Association, Washington, D.C., 1974.

Cardwell, Paul, Jr. *America's Camping Book.* Revised edition. New York: Charles Scribner's Sons, 1976.

Clegg, Peter. *New Low Cost Sources of Energy for the Home.* Charlotte, Vermont: Garden Way, 1975.

Coleman, Peter J. *Woodstove Know-How.* Charlotte, Vermont: Garden Way, 1974.

Cooper, Jane. *Woodstove Cookery.* Charlotte, Vermont: Garden Way, 1977.

Dow, George Francis. *Everyday Life in the Massachusetts Bay Colony.* Reissued, 1967. Boston: Benjamin Bloom Publishers, 1935.

Eastman, Margaret, and Wilbur F., Jr. *Planning and Building Your Fireplace.* Charlotte, Vermont: Garden Way, 1976.

Explorers Ltd. *Explorers Ltd. Source Book.* New and enlarged. New York: Harper & Row, 1977.

American Forestry Association. *Forest Service.* Washington, D.C.

Foxfire Books, Vols. #1, 2, 3, and 4 (Doubleday) Anchor Books, 1972 to 1977.

Gay, Larry. *The Complete Book of Heating with Wood,* Charlotte, Vermont: Garden Way, 1974.

Government Publications. Supt. of Documents, Washington, D.C.: *Fireplaces & Chimneys,* 1971, Cat. #PL-31 S/N, 3900–0143, 3:32 #132A, 20c per copy; *Home Maintenance,* PL-1972; *Campstoves & Fireplaces,* 1937, 50c per copy; Cat. # A13.2: C15/16 SNO101-0002; *Farmer's Bulletin,* #2090, USDA, Logging Farm Wood Crops; U.S. Forest Service, FPL-090-USDA-

Wood Fuel Preparation; *Farmer's Bulletin* #1889, USDA, "Fireplaces & Chimneys."

Groene, Janet. *Cooking on the Go.* New York: Grosset & Dunlap, 1971.

Kephart, Horace. *Camping & Woodcraft.* New York: Macmillan, 1972.

Langer, Richard. *Joy of Camping.* New York: Saturday Review Press, 1973.

Leonard, Jonathan N. *American Cooking—The Great West.* New York: Time-Life Books, 1971.

Loebel, Alice. *The Stockpot and Steamer Cookbook.* New York: Macmillan, 1966.

Lytle, R. J. and Marie-Jeanne. *Book of Successful Fireplaces.* Farmington, Michigan: Structures Publishing Co., 1971.

Marshall, Mel. *Cooking Over Coals.* New York: Winchester Press, 1971.

National Fire Protection Association, International, 470 Atlantic Avenue, Boston, MA. 02210. $2 per copy. NFPA, #89m, *Heat Producing Appliance Clearance,* 1971; NFPA, #10, *Extinguishers, Installation,* 1973; NFPA, #211, *Chimneys, Venting, 1972; NFPA, #HS-8, Using Coal and Wood Stoves Safely,* 1974.

Restino, Susan. *Mrs. Restino's Country Kitchen.* New York: Quick Fox, 1976.

Riviere, Bill. *Family Campers' Cookbook.* New York: Tower, 1965.

Self, Charles. *Buying and Installing a Woodstove.* Charlotte, Vermont: Garden Way, 1977 (Bulletin #A10).

Self, Charles. *Save $$ on Firewood.* Charlotte, Vermont: Garden Way, 1977 (Bulletin #A11).

Sunset Editors. *How to Plan and Build Your Fireplace.* Menlo Park, California: Sunset Books, 1973.

Vivian, John. *Wood Heat.* Emmaus, Pennsylvania: Rodale Press, 1976.

Index